W9-BKK-224

The High-Beta Rich

Also by Robert Frank
Richistan

The High-Beta Rich

HOW THE MANIC WEALTHY

WILL TAKE US TO THE

NEXT BOOM, BUBBLE, AND BUST

Robert Frank

CROWN
BUSINESS
NEW YORK

Published in the United States by Crown Business, an imprint of the Crown Publishing Group, a division of Random House, Inc., New York. www.crownpublishing.com

CROWN BUSINESS is a trademark and CROWN and the Rising Sun colophon are registered trademarks of Random House, Inc.

Crown Business books are available at special discounts for bulk purchases for sales promotions or corporate use. Special editions, including personalized covers, excerpts of existing books, or books with corporate logos, can be created in large quantities for special needs. For more information, contact Premium Sales at (212) 572-2232 or e-mail specialmarkets@randomhouse.com.

Grateful acknowledgment is made to Dan Sheridan for permission to use an excerpt from "Big Money Ruins Everything," words and music by Dan Sheridan, Aspen, CO. Reprinted by permission.

Library of Congress Cataloging-in-Publication Data

Frank, Robert, 1968–
The high-beta rich : how the manic wealthy will take us to the
next boom, bubble, and bust / Robert Frank.—1st ed.
p. cm.
Includes bibliographical references and index.
1. Wealth—United States. 2. Rich people—United States. 3. Millionaires—United States. 4. Business cycles—United States. 5. Recessions—United States. 6. Financial crises—United States. I. Title.
HC110.W4F735 2011
330.973'0931—dc23   2011019319

ISBN 978-0-307-58989-7
eISBN 978-0-307-58991-0

Printed in the United States of America

Book design by Robert Bull
Jacket design by Daniel Rembert
Jacket photography © Evox Images

10 9 8 7 6 5 4 3 2 1

First Edition

To Amelia and Elana

CONTENTS

vii

The High-Beta Rich

INTRODUCTION

Giving Up the Gulfstream

In the spring of 2006, at the glittering peak of America's Second Gilded Age, I flew to Palm Springs, California, to meet one of the nation's newest billionaires.

His name was Tim Blixseth. And, like many new billionaires at the time, he had more household staff than he could count. "Somewhere around a hundred" was his best guess at the time (it was actually 110). When I landed, I was greeted by one of his minions, a chipper Filipino chauffeur named Jesse, wearing khakis and a crisp white polo shirt, the universal uniform for helpers of the rich.

"Welcome, Mr. Frank!" Jesse said. "I'll be taking you to the residence."

Jesse and I climbed into his shiny black Land Rover, and he handed me a cold Fiji water and a lemon-scented towel from a cooler in the armrest. We pulled out of the airport and drove on Route 111, past the strip malls, car dealerships, and fast-food restaurants, and out toward the open desert. The sun was setting behind the orange peaks of the Santa Rosa Mountains, and a cool night breeze drifted across the valley from the Salton Sea. We turned onto a small road lined with neat rows of stucco homes and cactus gardens, and after about a mile the road came to an end at two wooden gates.

The gates soared more than twenty feet high, with intricate carvings of flowers and birds rising up giant block letters at the top that read: PORCUPINE CREEK.

Jesse picked up his handheld radio. "Car three with Mr. Frank now at property," he said.

A voice answered: "Entry granted, proceed."

The gates swung open to reveal a lush, water-filled wonderland—a stark contrast to the parched desert we were leaving behind.

The freshly washed driveway was lined with tropical flowers, palm trees, and antique French streetlamps that had once lined the Champs-Élysées. Streams and waterfalls gurgled alongside the road. Birds sang, and teams of gardeners, all wearing matching white polo shirts and khakis, waved as we passed by. When we reached the top of the first hill, Jesse slowed down to offer a view of a nineteen-hole golf course stretching for 240 acres at the foot of the mountains like a vast green welcome mat.

"Does he live in a golf community?" I asked Jesse.

Jesse laughed. "It's his golf course."

As I considered the practicality of owning and maintaining your own golf course in the middle of the desert, we pulled up to a circular driveway in front of an equally impressive display: a water fountain modeled after the famed Bellagio fountain in Las

Vegas ("but bigger," Blixseth insisted), shooting brightly lit arcs of water into the sky. Behind the fountain, the main house came into view—a sprawling Mediterranean mansion, rising over three stories with carved balconies, porticos, pillars, and large picture windows. It was lit by dozens of outdoor torches and surrounded by guest villas, pools, and gardens.

We pulled up to the imperial entry hall, where two life-size terra-cotta Chinese soldiers stood guard in front of a pair of bronze lions. The front door of the house opened, and out burst Tim—a smiling, compact man in a Hawaiian shirt and cargo shorts.

"Roberto!" he said, holding out a glass of Chardonnay. "Welcome to our humble abode. It's not much, but we call it home."

In 2006, Tim was little known outside a small circle of rich people in Palm Springs and California. But he was about to land on the *Forbes* list as one of the richest people in America, with an estimated net worth of $1.2 billion.

Tim and his outgoing blond wife, Edra, had made their fortune in timber and real estate. Their biggest trophy and their greatest source of wealth was the Yellowstone Club, a 10,000-acre private golf and ski resort nestled in the Montana Rockies that counted Bill Gates, cycling star Greg LeMond, and former vice president Dan Quayle as members, along with host of other recently rich corporate chiefs and finance executives. Officially, members had to have a minimum net worth of $7 million to join, but most were far richer, since they had to build a home at Yellowstone and buy land, which cost more than $2 million an acre. Once approved, they had the run of a golf course and ski area populated solely by fellow millionaires and billionaires. No one had to worry about the occasional non-rich interlopers you might encounter in, say, Aspen or Palm Beach. They enjoyed heated gondolas and

CEO-friendly ski trails with names such as "Learjet Glades" and "EBITDA" (a corporate term that means "earnings before taxes, depreciation, and amortization").

The Yellowstone Club was a huge success. By 2006, plots of land were selling for five times their original price. The club not only made Tim and Edra rich but also turned them into the unofficial innkeepers of the new elite, as they hosted the ultra-wealthy of Silicon Valley, Hollywood, Wall Street, and Washington. Porcupine Creek boasted wall after wall of photographs of the Blixseths with George Bush, Arnold Schwarzenegger, Gerald Ford, Mariel Hemingway, and other notables.

Their lifestyle was unapologetically excessive, even by the standards of the mid-2000s. They owned two yachts, three private jets, two Rolls-Royce Phantoms (his and hers), seven homes, a private island in the Caribbean, and a castle in France.

Porcupine Creek's staff of 110 maintained the home like a five-star resort. There was a kitchen staff of twelve manning five kitchens. There were towel boys by the pool, and waiters and chefs near every table or patio. One day, Tim was driving me around the golf course when a waiter popped up from behind a hedge to refill my wineglass. There were caddies, masseuses, security guards, drivers, gardeners, and technology experts to attend to every need.

They had a clubhouse with men's and women's locker rooms, a pro shop, and an equipment room—even though the Blixseths were sometimes the only players on the course, accompanied by their dogs named Learjet and G2 (for Gulfstream).

Every guest room and bathroom on the property was stocked with new bars of soap and robes emblazoned with the house logo, a smiling brown porcupine.

When I asked Edra why she needed to run her house like a

luxury resort, she was very matter-of-fact. "That's the way we've always done things, with five-star standards. The employees were happy to have the jobs and we were happy to employ them. There was just never any thought to costs."

Despite their imperial lifestyle, the Blixseths were friendly, funny, and fiercely driven. They threw epic parties, including $1 million weddings for their children and a $300,000 party for Tim's fiftieth birthday featuring a "living time machine" of famous rock bands and fashions from the past half century.

They were embodiments of the American dream. Tim grew up poor in rural Oregon, with what he calls "a rusty spoon in my mouth." He often tells the story of how other kids taunted him on the cafeteria line in high school: "Welfare kid, welfare kid!" Edra was a single mom at the age of seventeen and worked the night shift at a diner before she started her own business and eventually met Tim. Now they were billionaires, at least on paper.

The Blixseths were also typical of America's twenty-first-century wealth boom, in which real estate tycoons, entrepreneurs, and financiers could make colossal fortunes almost overnight with the right mix of luck, hard work, leverage, and asset bubbles. In 2006, when I was searching for people to profile for my book on the new American rich, the Blixseths seemed like naturals. I spent three days with them as they flitted from house to house and jet to yacht, as well as countless hours with them in follow-up interviews.

One evening Tim leaned back on the couch on the deck of his yacht and poured himself a glass of Chardonnay.

"Boy, if my dad could only see me now," he said. "He would never have dreamed I would have a life like this. It's been a wild ride."

As it turned out, the ride was about to get a lot wilder.

THE MIRAGE IN THE DESERT

In the winter of 2010 I flew back to Palm Springs. But this time there was no Jesse or Range Rover or lemon-scented towels.

I climbed into my rented Hyundai and drove out to Route 111 toward the Blixseths'. When I reached the wooden gates, I pressed the call button on the intercom. A recorded voice crackled over the loudspeaker: "This is a special message from Verizon. The service to this telephone has been temporarily disconnected."

I kept buzzing and kept getting the recording. A few minutes later I heard a golf cart buzz down the property driveway. The gates cracked open and out peered Edra, looking overtanned and overtired. Instead of her usual designer suit or skirt, she was wearing jeans and a sweatshirt.

"Hi there!" she said, beaming. "Welcome back! Sorry about the gate. They shut the phones off because I couldn't pay the bill."

Edra climbed into her muddy golf cart and told me to follow her to the house. "I'll give you the tour. You won't believe it. Or maybe you will. Did you ever see the movie *Grey Gardens*?"

We rolled our way up the driveway, which was littered with dead leaves and branches. The waves of flowers had turned into brown weeds, and the streams and waterfalls had all dried out, leaving trails of cracked concrete. The golf course had turned an anemic shade of yellow and was strewn with fallen palm branches. When we stopped to look out over the seventh hole, there was total silence. Even the birds had flown off to seek greener pastures.

As we reached the front of the house, the Bellagio fountain was now an algae-covered pool. The terra-cotta soldiers were still standing guard, but with the emptiness around them, they looked more like lost sentries who had somehow missed the order to retreat.

We made our way inside. The house looked frozen in time and caked in dust. The living room was still filled with burnished European antiques, brightly colored ceiling murals, French chandeliers, and photos of Edra with Hollywood celebrities and politicians. The home's health spa, gym, chef's kitchens, and regal dining room all looked just as they had four years earlier. The soap dishes were still filled with little soap cakes embossed with the smiling porcupine. But it was eerily still.

Edra had laid off the last of her household staff the week earlier. Keeping up 30,000 square feet of house was proving far too great a task for one woman. She shuffled around the house with a roll of paper towels and a bottle of Windex, wiping off the chairs and tables before she sat down.

We toured the garage, which once had housed the two Rolls-Royce Phantoms and the Aston Martin DB-9 that Tim gave Edra for an anniversary present. Now it housed Edra's golf cart and a ten-year-old Mercedes.

In the living room, a large fish tank stood on the center table. During my previous visit, the tank had been the room's shining centerpiece—a 100-gallon Technicolor panorama of coral, anemones, and rare tropical fish. Now most of the fish and coral were gone. All that remained were two clown fish swimming around a slab of concrete.

"What happened to the coral?" I asked Edra.

"It got repossessed," she said.

Edra explained that a local high-end aquarium company used to come and clean the tank and provide the coral, shells, and other ocean-scene accessories for about $1,200 a month. But after three months went by without payment, they took their coral and shells back.

"At least they left me the fish," she said with a smile.

As we sat down, Edra listed the other ways in which her life had changed. The Yellowstone Club had gone bankrupt and was sold, and she had filed for Chapter 7 personal bankruptcy. The Gulfstreams were gone, and she had auctioned off most of her jewelry and antiques. She and Tim were in the midst of a public and bitter divorce that had dragged on for more than three years, and most of her days were now spent in court or with lawyers, fighting off the dozens of lawsuits or investigations related to her financial collapse.

After decades of having her own household staff, Edra was doing her own cooking, cleaning, shopping, and driving.

"I just discovered this place called Marshalls yesterday," she told me. "Amazing! I had never been there. It's so cheap."

Losing the jets was the hardest part. After giving up the Gulfstreams, Edra made her first commercial flight in more than twenty years, on a trip to court in Montana. "It was horrible," she said. "The security search, it was demeaning. And I was late for the flight, but they wouldn't hold it for me. When I finally got on a flight, I got stuck in the very back seat between two other people. Nightmare."

As Edra and I walked back through the house, I stopped again at the fish tank. I flashed back to the boom times of 2006, when Tim and Edra had been on top of the world, among the four hundred richest people in America. They could fly on their Gulfstream 550 to their French castle for dinner and return for breakfast and golf with Bill Gates. Their staff was larger than the workforce of most businesses.

Yet by 2010, it all looked like another mirage in the California desert. The Edra I was standing next to was flat broke. Her phones had been shut off. Her staff was gone. The coral in her fish tank had been repossessed.

The Blixseths' success, like so much American wealth at the turn of the twenty-first century, was built on an illusion.

8

A NEW NATION

Between 1990 and 2007, America experienced its largest wealth boom in history. By 2007, there were more than ten million millionaire households in America, and more than half a million households worth more than $10 million—more than double the numbers in 1990.

Never before had so many people become so wealthy so fast. The Gilded Age of the late 1800s and the Roaring Twenties in the early twentieth century may have created richer individuals relative to the economy, with John D. Rockefeller's wealth equal to 1.5 percent of the entire U.S. gross domestic product (GDP), which would be equal to $210 billion today. Yet the Second Gilded Age of the 1990s and 2000s eclipsed all others when it came to the sheer number of new millionaires and billionaires. The combined annual incomes of the top 1 percent exploded to $1.7 trillion, greater than the annual GDP of Canada. Their wealth topped $21 trillion at its peak in 2007.

The soaring fortunes of the rich grew in stark contrast to the rising debts and stagnant wages of the rest of America. The rich seemed to have created a self-contained world of privilege and prosperity, with their own health care system (concierge doctors), education system (private schools), travel network (private jets), and language ("Have your family office call mine"). The American wealthy had created their own virtual country, a place I called Richistan.

In my book of the same name, I profiled the people, places, and status markers of this strange new land. I shadowed shampoo tycoons in Palm Beach, garbage-collection heiresses in California, and a Jewish Irishman in Texas who was using his tech millions to help the poor in Ethiopia. I chronicled the rising demand for everything from butlers and personal arborists to five-hundred-foot yachts and private jets equipped with alligator-skin toilet seats.

During the peak of the Second Gilded Age, in 2008, Richistan appeared unstoppable. The fortunes of the rich just kept climbing, becoming as monumental and seemingly permanent as the 30,000-square-foot fortresses they now called home.

They had achieved the economic version of escape velocity, breaking free of the usual financial forces of gravity that kept the rest of America on the ground and prone to downturns. Economists opined that if America had a crisis or recession, Richistan would barely feel the impact, like a G550 hitting a small air pocket, causing its well-heeled passengers to momentarily clutch their glass of '86 Mouton to avoid a spill before resuming their ride at 40,000 feet.

Then, in 2008, Richistan panicked.

In the eighteen-month period between 2008 and the middle of 2009, the fortunes of the nation's millionaires fell by about a third—marking the greatest one-time destruction of wealth since the 1930s. The population of American millionaires plummeted by more than 20 percent, effectively wiping out five years of growth. Richistan's lofty incomes also came tumbling down.

In percentage terms, the losses at the top surpassed those of any other income group in America. Incomes for the top 1 percent of earners fell three times as much as they did for American earners as a whole. The biggest losers were the super-earners, or those in the top one-tenth of 1 percent, who make $9.1 million or more per year. This elite group saw its income drop more than four times the average fall in the United States. As we will see, some of the wealthy—like Edra Blixseth—experienced almost unimaginable falls, as their net worth went from hundreds of millions of dollars to zero.

We shouldn't shed any tears for the expatriates of Richistan. Giving up their Gulfstreams and poolside waiters may qualify as emotional trauma for people like Edra Blixseth. Yet their fall to mere affluence is proof that all suffering is relative. As millions of non-rich Americans lose their jobs and homes, many of the rich are already recovering from the financial crisis, thanks in part to the government bailout of Wall Street and the Federal Reserve's support of financial markets and cheap money. As a reader of my *Wealth Report* blog wrote: "The rich have gotten back what they lost and the rest of America is still in the purple fart cloud of the last bust."

In fact, one of the lasting legacies of the Great Recession may be that Richistan was further removed from America. The stunning fall of the rich may have brought them momentarily closer to the non-rich. But Richistan seems more foreign than ever, as many Americans lose hope of ever getting rich themselves. In our post-TARP, deficit-ridden age, many see the rich as the winners in a zero-sum game of global wealth. Richistan and America are viewed more like Disraeli's "Two Nations," "between whom there is no intercourse and no sympathy, who are as ignorant of each other's habits, thoughts, and feelings as if they were dwellers in different zones . . . and not governed by the same laws."

Yet Richistan's ups and downs reveal a much deeper and more important change in our economy and in American wealth today—one that was laid bare by the Blixseths and countless others. Today's wealth is no longer secure or stable, but built on a global financial system that's increasingly prone to sudden shocks, crashes, and bubbles. While those shocks may seem irrelevant and even amusing to the rest of us, they will increasingly reverberate through our financial and political life as the rich dominate more and more of the economy and funding for governments.

Rather than viewing the financial crisis as a narrow escape for the rich, it may have been a warning that the worst is yet to come.

THE PAPER PLUTOCRACY

For the past eight years, I've been the wealth reporter for the *Wall Street Journal*, covering the lives and economy of the rich. I don't carry a flag in the class wars. I'm not out to celebrate or castigate the rich, or to write a partisan polemic (there are already plenty of those). My aim is to report on the world of wealth just as I covered foreign countries as an overseas correspondent—describing the facts and details on the ground to readers far away.

If I follow any faith, it is the guidance of the economist John Kenneth Galbraith, who wrote, "Of all the classes, the wealthy are the most noticed and the least understood." As our economy becomes increasingly dominated by the wealthy—by their incomes, their spending, their taxes, and their political influence—the rich merit understanding beyond the size of their mansions and private jumbo jets. We need to understand the basis of their fortunes, the deeper economic forces that lifted them to the top, and the changes that wealth has brought to their lives and values. By following the trajectory of the rich, who increasingly shape the direction of the rest of the country, we might be able to get a clearer picture of our own financial and political path.

In that spirit, I started reporting on the serial blowups of the super-rich during the financial crisis of 2008 and 2009. There were the Madoff victims, of course. And there were entrepreneurs such as the Bucksbaum family, whose shopping mall fortune plunged more than 95 percent, from $3 billion to about $100 million. Bankruptcies among the formerly rich reached all-time highs.

These weren't the usual stories we associate with wealth loss— the financially challenged lottery winners and extravagant celebrities who blow their windfalls on binges in Las Vegas and Ferraris for their friends. The big losers in 2008 and 2009 were self-made businesspeople who were supposed to know a thing or two about money.

As fascinating as they were, however, the tales of extreme financial loss didn't seem to merit a book. They were more like the Bugatti crashes that have become popular on YouTube—spectacular displays of wealth destruction that made for great schadenfreude but had little long-term meaning.

Then I discovered two remarkable charts.

They were created by Jonathan Parker and Annette Vissing-Jorgensen, both economists at Northwestern University, using data from the Internal Revenue Service. The charts showed the gains and losses of various income groups dating back to World War II.

Here is the first chart, which shows incomes during expansions for all taxpayers and for the top 1 percent:

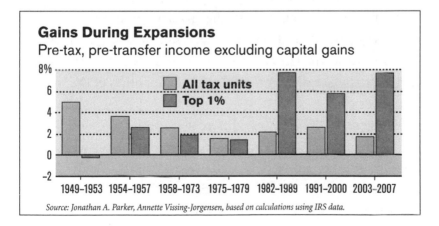

Gains During Expansions
Pre-tax, pre-transfer income excluding capital gains

Source: Jonathan A. Parker, Annette Vissing-Jorgensen, based on calculations using IRS data.

As you can see, the top 1 percent did far better than the rest of America during the recent boom times, telling the well-known story of rising inequality and the outsize gains of the few at the top.

Here is the other, more important chart. It shows the relative income losses during downturns:

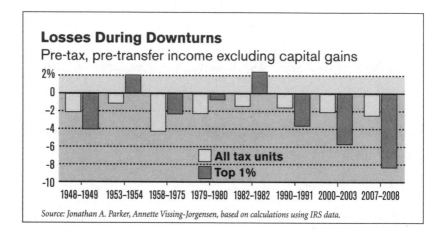

Losses During Downturns
Pre-tax, pre-transfer income excluding capital gains

Source: Jonathan A. Parker, Annette Vissing-Jorgensen, based on calculations using IRS data.

The chart shows that the top 1 percent led the country in income losses during the past three recessions. In the most recent downturn, the incomes of the elite sank more than twice as much as the rest of the country's.

Even more intriguing was the history of those losses. The chart suggests that the Great Recession was not, in fact, a one-off. It was the latest in a series of escalating income shocks that led to huge spikes and crashes in the incomes of the wealthiest Americans.

These serial crashes were different from the more traditional ebbs and flows of American wealth, where old money was shoved aside by the nouveaux riche and large fortunes usually took a lifetime (or even generations) to dissipate. These new cycles of wealth were much faster and more extreme. Rather than taking three generations to make and lose a fortune, as expressed in the old adage of "shirtsleeves to shirtsleeves in three generations," today's rich were completing the cycle in a decade or less.

Risk has always been the handmaiden to large wealth. And there have always been rich people who look far richer than they really are, embodied by the saying "all hat and no cattle." Still, the outsize losses and gains of the wealthy marked something new in our economy. For nearly four decades after World War II, the top 1 percent was the steady line on America's income chart, gaining less and losing less than the rest of America during economic cycles. In the early 1980s—1982, to be precise—the top 1 percent broke away and became the most unstable force in the economy.

The research put the recession and the wealthy in a new light. An elite that had once been models of financial sobriety suddenly set off on a wild ride of economic binges. The trusty "millionaires next door," with their rusty Ford pickup trucks, cheap suits, and hypercautious savings habits, had been eclipsed by a strange new personality type in the world of wealth. They were more manic in their earnings and spending, and they were by-products of a new system of financial incentives that rewarded extreme risk-taking, borrowing, speculation, and spending.

I call them the high-beta rich. In financial markets, the term *high-beta* usually refers to a stock that experiences exaggerated swings relative to the broader market. Tech stocks and start-ups, for instance, usually have a high beta. The high-beta rich had become like the human tech stocks of our economy, prone to violent swings and rapid cycles of value creation and destruction.

To me, this new personality type and the changing character of American wealth have largely gone undiscovered. This book aims to chronicle the rise and occasional fall of the high-beta rich and how they impact the rest of us.

———

THE AGE OF HIGH-BETA WEALTH

The rise of the high-beta rich is important for three reasons.

First, the losses of the rich offer important lessons for all of us. While the story of getting rich has become a tired cliché in American culture, from Horatio Alger to Mark Zuckerberg, tales of losing large wealth are more rare but arguably just as important. Losing large amounts of wealth can offer a fresh perspective on what really matters in life. Without the trappings of money and power, the rich sometimes gain a better appreciation of their true friends, of their work or their passions, and of their connections to other people and communities—all of which can be obscured by wealth. They learn how quickly the things that once seemed so important (from jets and mansions to lavish parties and social status) can quickly vanish.

For some, of course, going from riches to rags is a nightmare from which they hope to awaken. They just want their jets and parties back. Yet to others, it is a crash course in learning to live more with less.

We can also gain financial wisdom from the fall of the rich. Since we often learn best from extremes, stories of radical wealth loss can show us how to better manage and perserve our own finances—from controlling our spending and understanding our investments to preparing for a crisis and borrowing money. (Lesson One: You're only as smart as your debts).

In the coming chapters, you'll meet a midwetern excavator who became a millionaire and found his dream retirement, only to be forced to sell his Florida estate at the bottom of the market. Today he lives in a truck. You'll meet a family who built the biggest house in America, then ran out of cash and had to put the house up for sale. We will learn more about Edra Blixseth and her astonishing journey from billionaire to bust.

Along the way, I'll ask questions both serious and trivial. What happens to the rich when they lose the money that defines them? If money can't buy happiness, does losing great wealth make us happier or twice as miserable? How does someone employ, let alone fire, a household staff of 110 people?

The second reason we should care about high-beta wealth is because it reveals a new and untold side of the American upper class. The stereotypes of today's rich usually include fat-cat Wall Street bankers who never miss a bonus, or thrifty small-business owners who scrimped and saved their way to wealth. Both types exist, of course. But today's wealthy are wilder and more diverse than ever. Most of the super-rich made their money by starting and selling a company. Others became millionaires by running a publicly traded company or rising to the top of their field in law, medicine, science, or entertainment. Yet the rich today have one thing in common: their wealth is increasingly linked to financial markets, either through the companies they started and sold, or through huge salaries paid with shares or options. The way to get super-rich is no longer by making things or owning a family business, but from stock, deals, financial engineering, and "liquidity events." These cash windfalls make entrepreneurs and financiers fabulously wealthy, but also make them vulnerable to booms, bubbles, and busts.

In the coming pages, you'll meet two brothers who grew up on the cargo docks of New Jersey and became billionaires from building up their family shipping business. Even the toughest dock workers in New Jersey, however, couldn't prepare them for the wealth managers of Wall Street and the hundreds of millions of dollars they lost in just a few months. You will meet a family whose fortune started with a flock of German canaries and grew to include a real estate empire and hedge fund, showing how wealth has migrated from the real to the financial.

We will also see how the wealthy are borrowing and spending more than ever before, projecting an image of success in front of a mountain of debt.

Behind their new Feadship yachts, Bentleys, and Tudor-tropical mountain ranches, many of today's rich are only one crisis away from losing it all. They form a Potemkin plutocracy ever fearful of being exposed. In the next chapter, you will meet the grim reaper of this overextended overclass: a luxury repo man who nabs private jets and yachts that are in financial default. These stories challenge our perception that it is only the middle class and poor who binged on debt and who are susceptible to downturns.

The third and most important reason to learn about high-beta wealth is its impact on our future. The growing gap between the rich and the rest, with America's top 1 percent controlling more than a third of the country's wealth, means that the wealthy have growing economic influence and power—a trend well documented in books such as *Wealth and Democracy,* by Kevin Phillips; *The Winner-Take-All Society,* by Robert H. Frank (no relation); and *Winner-Take-All Politics,* by Jacob Hacker and Paul Pierson.

The rise of high-beta wealth introduces a new side effect of inequality: With the growing dominance of the rich has come growing contagion from their financial manias. In the coming pages, we will see how high-beta wealth is wreaking havoc on the consumer economy, our financial markets, and even state governments. You will meet an economist who worked for the California state government and tried for years to warn politicians about the state's dangerous dependence on the volatile incomes of the rich. When his warnings were ignored, California fell into its worst budget crisis in history, due in large part to the evaporating incomes of the state's tech tycoons.

You will see how the spending of the rich has become five times more volatile than their incomes. As the wealthy account for more and more of our economy, with the top 5 percent of American earners accounting for 37 percent of consumer outlays, the American economy will also experience more extreme cycles. You will see the human impacts of this high-beta spending, including an unemployed butler who was forced to hang up his silver tray when his millionaire employer had to downsize.

We shouldn't feel sympathy for the roller-coaster rich. But we should worry for the rest of the country. If the national risks of high-beta wealth had a simple equation, it would look like this:

America's dependence on the rich + great volatility among the rich = a more volatile America.

As go the high-beta wealthy, so goes the rest of the country. While trickle-down economics may be widely dismissed as a myth, I will show in the following pages how trickle-down losses are already becoming a reality.

To research this book, I interviewed more than a hundred people with net worths (or former net worths) of $10 million or more. While the people I've profiled are among the most colorful and interesting in the group, they are representative of the larger sample in their experiences and perspective. The profiles are based on on-the-record interviews with each subject (some totaling seventy hours or more over the course of two years) as well as secondary reporting and research.

We begin our journey with an economic species normally seen in low-income neighborhoods or lurking behind suburban garages after midnight. He is the repo man.

PART I

———●———

*The Rise of High-Beta
Wealth*

1

WHO REPO'D MY YACHT?

The smell of espresso and freshly baked croissants fills the private-jet terminal of Orlando Sanford International Airport. A businessman in a tailored gray suit sits on the suede couch of the lounge, reading the *Economist* and waiting for his Gulfstream to refuel. A family in Bermuda shorts and polo shirts, carrying their fluffy white Maltese, parades out the door to their NetJets plane on their way to the Caribbean.

It's another peaceful morning in the rarified world of the private-jet set. Then Ken Cage barges through the door.

He is stout and quick, with a slight potbelly hanging over his jeans and a Phillies cap pulled low on his forehead. He is the only person in the lounge with a goatee. As Ken waves to the startled receptionist, the businessman clutches his briefcase. The NetJets family scurries faster toward their plane. Cage bounds through the terminal and opens a glass door that leads to the tarmac.

Following close behind him is Randy Craft, a six-foot-two former professional wrestler with a shaved head and tattoos. He has a black Ford F-150 with the words "The Bone Collector" inscribed on the steering wheel.

In the hot Florida sun, Ken and Randy walk along the concrete apron and scan the line of planes parked in a neat row alongside the terminal. They home in on a shiny white Cessna 515, with silver propellers and a red racing stripe.

Ken pulls out a sheet of paper and reads out a series of letters and numbers. Randy scans the numbers on the plane's tail fin.

"That's our baby," says Randy.

Ken's BlackBerry beeps. It's an urgent text sent from one of his secret informers nearby—either a mechanic or a fuel guy, Ken won't say. Ken reads the text. "Cessna to depart to Mexico at noon. Owner tipped off, on way back to airport. Owner is six foot six." Ken looks at Randy. "Six foot six?" he says. "I don't want to stick around for that."

Ken looks at his watch. It's 11:57 a.m.—leaving them exactly three minutes until he's face-to-face with a pissed-off, NBA-size airplane owner.

Randy runs over to the plane and starts picking the lock on the door. Within seconds he's got it open, and he lowers the stairway. Ken's pilot, a fearless crop duster and stunt pilot who has just come onto the apron, rushes over to the plane and jumps in. After a cursory safety check (Wings? Check. Engines? Check) the pilot starts the engines, and the propellers roar to life. In two minutes he's careening off the apron and onto the taxiway. After getting clearance from the tower, he guns the plane down the runway and hits the air at exactly 11:59.

Randy looks at his watch "Plenty of time. We still have thirty seconds left."

Randy and Ken run back through the terminal and hop into their Ford pickup truck. As they tear out of the parking lot, a black Bentley with a tall, silver-haired driver roars down the entrance road toward the terminal. Ken ducks in his seat as the car races past.

When the coast is clear, he pops his head up and looks back. "I could use a beer."

Randy cranks up the radio and puts on his Texas Longhorns baseball cap. "That was an easy one. Wait till you hear about the yacht we're about to get."

Ken Cage and Randy Craft are repo men of Richistan. While other repo men take cars and trucks from the poor and lower middle class, Ken and Randy take private jets, helicopters, yachts, and racehorses from the overextended wealthy. They are the scavengers of high-beta wealth, picking up the shiny remains of a decade's worth of conspicuous consumption financed with debt, asset bubbles, and soaring stock prices.

In their three years in business, they've have been shot at, assaulted, run over by a car, and nearly strangled by an ex-NFL linebacker. While they are hardly popular with the formerly rich, they have become a necessary part of the new life cycle of wealth, where today's millionaires are tomorrow's deadbeats.

In 2009, Ken's company, Orlando-based International Recovery Group, repossessed more than seven hundred boats, planes, helicopters, and other wealth trophies (he calls them "units"). The combined worth of that year's catch was more than $100 million, up sixfold from 2007, and he says 2011 and 2012 could be even better.

The main reason? The rise of high-beta wealth.

Ken says most of his targets are highfliers who made their money in real estate, financial markets, or business. When their rising debts caught up with the plunging values of their assets, they experienced what the well-heeled like to refer to as a "short-term liquidity issue." In other words, they were out of cash.

"The big thing is that people made money quickly and went hog wild," he says. "They didn't realize that the highs at some point become lows. They just thought this wave would roll forever. Well, guess what? It crashes too. And they still haven't learned their lesson, even after this shit storm we've been through. I hate to say it, but I'm going to be in business a long time."

Sudden wealth loss has become a profitable business for elite repo men such as Ken and Randy. They've created a cottage industry around the shattered lifestyles of the rich, and their ranks are growing. Most of today's other high-end repo men specialize in one area, whether it's planes or yachts or Lamborghinis. Nick Popovich, the self-described "big-game hunter" of Indiana, has nabbed more than fifteen hundred planes in his career and says "business has never been better."

Ken Hill of Santa Barbara, California, whose friends call him "the Grim Reaper," has repossessed hundreds of planes since taking his first Piper Cherokee in 1969. He travels at a moment's notice and carries just a few essentials—a propeller lock, a portable radio, a handheld GPS, and a fanny pack stuffed with hundreds of keys.

Jeff Henderson, a Michigan-based repo man who targets boats, told the *New York Times* that he has a number of repeat offenders, or people who get the same boat repossessed multiple times as they've lost a fortune, made it back, then lost it again.

"One guy, I took his boat four times," he said.

The private-jet and yacht craze of the past fifteen years was driven by the explosion in multimillionaires and easy loans from banks. Between 1995 and 2010, the number of private jets in the air more than doubled, from 7,176 to 17,199. With prices of private jets falling by more than half, many jet owners who used borrowed money are now upside down on their plane finances, leading to rising loan defaults.

Some of the more public defaulters include Minnesota auto dealer Denny Hecker, who built an empire of GM and Chrysler dealerships and bought a twenty-two-seat Hawker private plane with $12.8 million borrowed from a finance unit of General Electric. He borrowed an additional $357,196 against the plane shortly after the purchase. When his business tanked, the lender repo'd the plane. Hecker's yacht was also repossessed as part of his fruitless efforts to pay back $767 million in debts.

The vagaries of the rich have created other new kinds of business as well. A national chain of pawnshops, called Boomerang Lending, has grown rapidly over the past few years by focusing on the affluent. Wealthy debtors hock Rolexes and Rolls-Royces in exchange for up to $200,000 in cash. Rather than walking into a dingy pawnshop and risk being seen, they can ship their items or drop them off at a discreet office.

"There is a certain type of affluent customer that will not go into a pawnshop," said founder Todd Hills. "And they don't have a $50 or $100 problem. Maybe they have a $100,000 problem."

Recessions have always claimed their share of rich people living on the edge. But high-end repo men say that the past three recessions—for reasons we'll examine in the next chapter—have each claimed successively larger numbers of rich people, with successively larger paper fortunes.

"For us, 2008 was much better than 2000, and 2000 was better than 1990," Popovich says. "Each time we get a recession, the private jets we're taking just get bigger."

He said there are airport hangars in Pennsylvania, Michigan, and Indiana filled with mothballed jets that were repo'd by banks. Since many planes were bought with balloon loans, with interest rates that start low and surge higher after five years, those loans are now starting to default.

The skies are filled with an even larger fleet of so-called zombie jets—jets that are in default but haven't been repo'd by banks. Popovich says it's often cheaper for the banks to take a hit on the loans than to repo the planes and pay for insurance and maintenance until the plane can be sold.

"Given the decline in aircraft values, the banks are getting nervous about pulling these planes back," Popovich says. "You've got planes that people bought for $8 million with an $8 million loan, and now the plane is worth $3.5 million. It's sometimes easier for the banks to just work out a deal with the owners."

Popovich still isn't worried: "I've got enough business that I now find myself telling the banks to hold off on repos."

THE THRILL OF THE CHASE

Like most luxury repo men, Ken Cage fell into his profession by accident. He grew up in rural Pennsylvania, the son of a middle-class family in a middle-class town. His dad owned a trucking company that delivered paper towels and toilet paper from the local Scott Paper plant.

"Everyone was in the same economic boat," he says. "A guy was super-rich in my town if he had $10 more than anyone else. I'm kidding, but you know what I mean. Everyone lived in the same kind of split-level ranch house with the same white aluminum siding. There wasn't a big difference between anybody."

Ken's dream was to play baseball or maybe become a math teacher. He loved math and had an unusual talent for numbers and statistics. He also played some semi-pro baseball. But after

Ken graduated from high school, his father died. Instead of going to college, he decided to go to work.

"My dad's death just kind of changed everything for me," Cage said.

He worked as a bank teller for a while, then found a job at a hazardous waste site in New Jersey. For eight to twelve hours a day, he shoveled mounds of contaminated soil and medical waste into a giant incinerator. Ken got married and had two kids.

The money was good. But eventually he decided he wanted more out of life than shoveling hazardous waste into a scorching furnace. He enrolled at a nearby commuter college and got a degree in math, later earning a place in the national mathematics honor society.

Ken bounced around from job to job and eventually landed as head of security for a Pennsylvania hospital. Most hospital security chiefs just watched the doors. But Ken launched his own internal investigation unit. He blew open two mini crime rings in the hospital, including one employee who was stealing computer chips and another who was stealing equipment.

Ken was thrilled by the task of rooting out bad guys, and he found a certain mathematical beauty in investigations.

"An investigation is very similar to math. It's all logic, where you learn the steps and the variables in order to put a case together," he says. "But this was a lot more fun."

He went on to work for Chrysler Financial, the Chrysler unit that handed out loans to its car buyers. He wound up in the high-risk collections department, dealing with customers who were more than thirty days late paying their car loans.

Ken says he learned two things from the collections department. "The first thing was that here are some people who are just financially stuck, and that's okay. You learn to be sympathetic to them. You work with them. Most of the time they're in a bad economic situation that's not their fault.

"The second thing I learned was that the lending practices in this country are totally screwed up."

Ken saw the loan documents for people who were late with payments and realized that many had never filled in the line indicating their occupation. Others didn't have an address or list any source of income.

When the German CEO of Chrysler Financial visited the offices, Ken asked him how the company could continue giving away such cheap, easy money.

"He said they were working on it, but that it would be hard to change," Ken recalls. "All my co-workers looked at me like I was crazy for asking the question. But to me it was obvious that they were going to have a problem." Working in high-risk collections meant handling repossessions. Ken didn't actually do any repos. But he assigned them, and most important, he answered the calls from people who had just had their cars repossessed.

"That breaks your heart. I mean, you got a mom who had her minivan taken while she was at work, with the child seats still inside. And she can't get home or pick up her kids. That's really tough."

Ken looked around for a more promising career. He and a golfing buddy started browsing business-broker sites, looking for a small business to buy. He found his dream: a high-end repo company in Florida that grabbed planes and boats from delinquent rich people. Ken could reap the benefits of the repo business without the heartbreaking calls from the minivan moms.

Ken's partner loved the idea. Ken's wife didn't. "She thought I'd get killed," Ken said. "She vetoed."

Ken abandoned his repo dream. A few months later, he and his wife were sitting on the couch watching TV and saw a show featuring a repo guy taking a plane in Alaska. It looked quick, safe, and easy.

"We looked at each other and said, 'That didn't look too bad. How hard could it be?'" Ken smiles. "I don't need to tell you, but TV can be misleading."

THE ANGRY RICH

There is an art to taking the prized possessions of the rich. After taking hundreds of yachts and planes, Ken has come up with some useful insights into the mind of the indebted millionaire. While repossessing from the poor or middle class requires muscle, stealth, and speed, the key to repossessing from the rich is to soothe their wounded egos.

"With the rich, it's all about pride and control. They're used to getting their way. So if they confront me while I'm taking their boat or plane, I say, 'I'm so sorry, sir. There must be a misunderstanding with the bank. I'm sure you've made your payments and there's been some terrible clerical error. So I'm just going to move this boat to storage until you can clear it up with the bank. Then we'll be happy to bring it back.' These rich guys know they've defaulted. And I know they've defaulted. But I never say it. So they say, 'Ah, right. Well, yes, it's a misunderstanding. Take it to storage for the time being and I'll clear it up later.' They lose the boat, but they save face. That's what they really care about more than the money."

Some rich people require a more direct approach.

"There are guys who say, 'You're not going to get my plane.' And I say, 'Oh yes I will.' It's me against the debtor, and he's not going to win."

Ken tells the story about the time he and Randy went to grab a yacht from a Cuban real estate tycoon in Florida.

"We go and we snoop around his mansion and see the yacht behind his house, docked in his private marina. So we rush in and grab it and start motoring down the Intracoastal Waterway. All of a sudden I look back and there's the guy, chasing us in another boat. I don't know if he had a gun or what, but he was approaching us real fast and screaming his head off. I call the Coast Guard, and they get there right as he's pulling up alongside us. The Coast Guard pulls him over, and we kept going. That was scary. But the funny thing is, I eventually repo'd his other boat as well. You can run, but you can't hide."

He mentions the time he thought he was about to be shot over a private jet.

"We're taking this Challenger jet and the pilot is a former NFL player who had become a pilot for the owner. He was huge. He was also a coke addict. So we were taking the plane and he comes out and jumps onto the plane and starts attacking us, punches our pilot, and says he has a gun. We eventually contacted the owner and got him calmed down. I felt sorry for the guy. The plane was his livelihood and we were threatening that."

When rich people turn bad, Ken turns to his hulking sidekick, Randy. Randy was a United World Wrestling star who went by the name "Rockin' Randy" and was known for his signature versions of the piledriver and the figure-four leg hold. When it comes to high-end repos, Randy Craft has two other essential skills: he can pick just about any lock in the world, and he knows the art of staged combat.

"One day I send Randy to Minnesota to get a plane in the middle of the winter, and he's walking to the hangar and the owner drives up in his car and starts heading right for Randy. Well, with the wrestling background, Randy was able to jump on the hood of the car and roll over the top without getting hurt. But the guy thought he'd killed him. So he freaked out and apologized. He was easier to deal with after that."

Ken has sad stories too—not like the ones from Chrysler, but still sympathetic. He was taking a boat from behind a house one summer day and a friendly woman came out to ask if he needed help.

"I started to tell her why I'm there, and she was very understanding. So we get to talking and she tells me that when housing prices were good, she bought a second house as an investment. She flipped it, made money, and bought two more. She said she only planned to have two or three properties, but pretty soon she had fifteen, and the boat and cars and all the rest. I told her I felt bad. But she said, 'Don't be sorry. It's all my fault. I should have known better. We all should have known better.' I thought that was pretty honest."

Ken and Randy even get the occasional words of praise from their targets. Hanging above Ken's computer in his spare, concrete-walled office near Orlando is a letter from a man who had his boat taken back by Ken and Randy.

> To whom it may concern:
>
> Reference: 2007 Angler
>
> A repossession is a very humiliating experience, particularly when one is generally a responsible human being. This sentence is an oxymoron because logic would question a "responsible human being" being in the same sentence as "repossession." Nonetheless a series of events that will only bore you will not be explained here, but rather I would like to commend your company on one of your lead investigators, Randy Craft.
>
> The referenced boat was repossessed from my home today. I was extremely surprised at Mr. Craft's demeanor. He was as

polite and respectful as he could be, while trying to obtain information and get his job done. He never gave an attitude, or was rude, or portrayed himself in any way that would have made an already bad and traumatic experience any worse.

We will try to get our boat back, but the main objective of this email is to let you know that Mr. Randy Craft should be commended on handling such an awkward, stressful, traumatic, emotional situation in the best possible manner—by treating the impacted person as a human being.

THE BIG FISH

When Ken bought his repo business from a previous owner in 2005, he expected to make a modest but steady income. During the first two years, he and Randy kept themselves busy scooping up single-engine propeller planes, twenty-foot fishing boats, personal watercraft, and the occasional broken-down helicopter.

He would clean up the repossessions and sell them at auction, keeping a percentage of the proceeds as profit and sending the rest back to the bank that held the loan.

"It was a nice, steady business," he says, "like reeling in small fish off the docks."

In late 2007 he got a giant tug on the line.

"One day I'm sitting in the office and I get a call from a bank for a plane job on the West Coast. I'm taking down the loan information and then the guy says 'GII.' As in Gulfstream II. I kind of paused for a minute because that's a $15 million plane. Until that point, all of our planes were Pipers and maybe a Cessna worth a couple hundred thousand. But the idea that we were repo'ing a Gulfstream was shocking. I mean, that's someone who once had $15 million to spend on a plane and now was now out of cash."

After that, he started getting more jets. The boats also got bigger, from little cruisers to full-size yachts. The average value of Ken's repossessions before the crisis was between $30,000 and $50,000. By 2010, the average value soared to between $300,000 and $500,000. He was not only doing more repossessions. His repossessions were also far more valuable, and he was taking them from people who are much wealthier—or at least they used to be.

Ken credits the banks for part of his newfound prosperity. During the boom times of the mid-2000s, banks loaned money to the wealthy at a record pace for homes, yachts, planes, art, cars, and even horses. Many banks would lend 100 percent of the value for a plane or boat, meaning buyers could sometimes walk away with a $20 million Gulfstream without putting down a single cent.

"There was an assumption that the rich had plenty of money, so why not lend them money," said so and so. "I mean, what could go wrong?"

A lot, as it turns out. Whenever he gets a job from a bank, Ken looks at the loan history. He usually discovers that the loan amounts are much larger than the property was ever worth.

Sifting through a pile of loan documents in his office one day, Ken ticks off a list of ill-considered loans. There's a Sea Ray boat he's about to repossess. The owner received a $240,000 loan to buy it at a time when the book value was under $200,000. Next Ken pulls out a sheet for a Cessna, purchased with a $345,000 loan at a time when the plane was worth $300,000.

"The lending practices are ridiculous. Why would a bank do that? How does that make sense?"

The main reason was deal flow. Like subprime mortgages, loans to the rich generated huge fees to bankers and lenders, regardless of the eventual outcomes. Loans were also a great way to win more profitable investment-advisory business from the wealthy. The rich would take out a jet loan, then give the bank their $200 milllion to manage. Banks figured the rich would always have money to pay back their loans because, well, they were rich.

What they failed to take into account was the rise of high-beta wealth. Many of the the new millionaires were borrowing to support their businesses and lifestyles. They were also products of an ever-rising real estate bubble and stock market. When both markets tanked, some of the rich had little or no cushion. In 2009, the number of defaults on plane loans more than doubled compared to 2008. Boat-loan defaults jumped fourfold the same year.

"They were no different from the rest of us," Ken says. "They just figured that if the wealthy were spending all this money, they had plenty more in the bank or in assets. But they didn't. A lot of these guys were living right on the edge, even though they seemed super-rich."

In the early days of the crisis, most of his business was concentrated around Florida, which was crawling with real estate developers, agents, and house flippers. By 2010, however, Ken was flying all over the country for repossessions and chasing down everyone from fallen tech titans in Silicon Valley to unemployed Wall Streeters in the Hamptons. High-beta wealth, Ken noticed, was now everywhere.

ABANDON YACHT!

On a humid morning, Ken walks along the creaky docks of the Big Isle Marina near Orlando. The parking lot is strewn with rusted-out fishing boats, sailboats turned on their side, and old wooden hulls with gaping holes, giving the marina the feel of a nautical graveyard. A morning mist floats along the top of the St. Johns River and unfurls behind the mangrove trees and Spanish moss.

Ken stands at the edge of the dock and looks down at a row of gleaming white boats tied to their berths. There's a sixty-six-foot Ocean Sport Fisherman, with shiny chrome railings, three levels, and high-tech fishing gear. There's a sleek thirty-eight-foot Concept center console with orange racing flames painted on the side, and a thirty-nine-foot Luhrs Open with a custom gangway.

All of the boats have been repossessed in recent months and all are now for sale. After Ken and Randy take the boats, they're brought here for repairs and cleaning. They sell most of the boats on their website for about half of the original purchase price.

Ken has a similar resting place for his planes—a nearby airfield with more than a dozen turboprops, jets, and helicopters grounded for lack of funds. As he walks down a line of planes, he taps each plane on the nose and offers a brief history: "Florida real estate agent . . . Las Vegas developer . . . tech guy . . ."

He adds, "I wonder how many of these planes I'll see again one day. I bet some will be back."

After grabbing the Cessna in Orlando, Ken and Randy set off on their next hunt. They drive toward Ocala National Forest, a vast stretch of pinelands laced with swamps, rivers, inlets, and creeks northwest of Orlando. It's a perfect place to hide a boat. Today they're looking for a sixty-five-foot Sea Ray that's in default. One of their informants, a local dock worker, gave them a tip that it might be nearby.

Ken and Randy have tipsters all over the country, from ground-crew workers at airports and receptionists at private-jet terminals to tugboat captains and marina workers. They say they rarely pay the tipsters, "except for the occasional beer. They help us because they think it's fun," Randy says.

In the search for the Sea Ray, they drive up to a small marina near Eustis and casually make their way along the docks. They wave hello to another boat owner and a dock worker, as if they're setting off for a morning sail. No one knows they're repo men.

The Sea Ray's not there. They try another marina. Nothing. Then a third and fourth. They're about to give up for the day when Randy gets an e-mail from his office. One of his boat captain friends has called in with a tip.

"The guy said a boat came into Hontoon Landing in the middle of the night last night with no lights," Randy tells Ken.

"No lights?" Ken asks

"No lights," Randy says.

Ken explains that there are only two reasons why boats around Ocala would cruise without lights: either they're running drugs or they're running from repo men. They race over to Hontoon, a well-manicured marina lined with large sport-fishing boats and party barges. A male rowing team, dressed in matching white spandex and baseball hats, have just finished their morning row. "Nice shorts," Randy chuckles.

Ken and Randy walk onto the dock and start inspecting the boats. They pass two Sea Rays, but neither is their target. They walk down to one end, then the other. No luck. At the very end of the dock, Randy spots the tip of a boat moored around the corner. It's blue and white, with a long bow platform, just like the one they're looking for. They glance around to make sure no one else is coming, then walk toward the boat. Randy jumps on first and lands on the rear deck. He opens the door to the galley and peers inside.

"Anyone home?" he calls. "Hello, hello?"

There's no answer. Kens jumps on, and they start looking for the boat's registration number, which Randy finds near the engine room. "This is our boat," he says. "Let's move."

Ken sits down in the control room and notices a cup of coffee, still hot, sitting on the galley counter. The owner, he says, is probably close by.

They crank up the engines, and Randy jumps out and unties the ropes. They check the fuel and start motoring down the river.

Once they're clear of the marina, Ken sits back in a plush leather chair on the main bridge and soaks up the sun. White egrets and pelicans glide along the shore, and a pair of fishermen bob nearby in a rowboat. Ken cracks open a bottle of water and enjoys a brief moment of quiet. He knows his cell phone will soon start ringing, with another job or an angry target.

But for now, Ken Cage is riding on the top deck of a Sea Ray, enjoying the life of an occasional boat owner.

"Someday I'd like to get my own boat," he says. "I almost bought one last year, but my wife said no. She thought it was a waste of money. But this is pretty nice. I could get used to this. I tell you one thing: If I bought one, I'd pay all cash."

Ken says he's not rich enough to buy his own yacht with cash—at least not yet. But as we'll see in the next chapter, the American rich are changing in ways that likely will keep Ken Cage in boats and planes for years to come. While 2008 and 2009 may have been banner years for the repo men of Richistan, their best payday is yet to come.

2

1982: THE MAGIC YEAR FOR WEALTH

The year 1982 rarely gets much attention in the lineup of magic years. Unlike 1968, 1941, or 1929, 1982 didn't usher in any cultural revolutions or wars or economic cataclysms. In 1982, President Ronald Reagan was struggling through his second year in office, with his popularity sinking and the country wallowing in economic recession. The unemployment rate was creeping up to 10 percent, and more than twelve million Americans were out of work. Interest rates were at 14 percent, leading to widespread business closures and bank failures.

Nineteen eighty-two wasn't the "morning in America" we would later associate with Reagan. It was more like the darkness before the dawn, with many economists and politicians doubting that Reagan's promises of trickle-down economics and growth fueled by tax cuts and deregulation would ever materialize.

As Kevin Phillips, the political commentator and former Republican strategist, wrote in his book *Wealth and Democracy*, 1982 was grim for just about all income groups in every part of the country. "The Farm Belt was in trouble, and the Great Lakes industrial region was smarting under its new, dismissive nickname: the Rust Belt. By the end of the year, median family income had slipped back to its 1974–75 lows."

New research, however, is shining a new light on 1982. Rather than being a year of false hopes, it may have been the crucible for America's Second Gilded Age. It was a year that set in motion a series of political and economic changes that would create the greatest wave of prosperity in nearly a century.

It also marked the birth of high-beta wealth.

To understand these changes and to see how the rise in inequality is tied to the rise of high-beta wealth we first have to go back in history to the pre-1982 world of wealth.

THE GREAT COMPRESSION

For nearly thirty years after World War II, the American wealthy were a small, quiet, and financially conservative group. They were removed from the nation's boisterous booms and busts and relatively restrained in their earning and spending. There was plenty of wealth created in America during the postwar years. But it didn't pile up at the top the way it did after 1982. Wealth was more broadly shared, thanks to high taxes on the wealthy, strong unions, New Deal programs, protectionist trade policies, and the nation's manufacturing power. America celebrated middle-class values and the "organization man." Big, quasi-paternalistic companies held the real wealth and power in America, rather than the individual entrepreneur or corporate executive. From a wealth perspective, 1947 to 1982 was the sturdy bridge built by the working class, straddling the wealth peaks of the Roaring Twenties and the years after 1982.

The wealthy sat on the sidelines as the economy ebbed and flowed. During the consumer-led expansion of the 1950s and the "nifty fifty" stock craze of the 1960s—in which investors piled into fifty popular stocks—the incomes and wealth of the top 1 percent barely kept pace with the rest of the population's. The average income of the bottom 90 percent of the population doubled between 1943 and 1980 in constant dollars, while the average income of the top 1 percent grew only 23 percent between 1943 and 1980, from $270,000 to $333,000.

The elite were equally restrained during downturns. During recessions in the 1960s and 1970s, the incomes of the top 1 percent fell less than the incomes for the rest of the country.

The pre-1982 rich, in other words, had a low beta, or low income-volatility compared to the rest of the country.

The population of rich people was also small. After the trauma of the Great Depression, which slashed the number of millionaires by more than 85 percent (and which we'll examine later), the rich were more like the shining city on the hill rather than the teeming nation we would later know as Richistan. In 1955, only 276 people made $1 million or more, compared to 513 in 1929.

Most wealth came from one of two sources: oil and trust funds. By some estimates, inherited wealth accounted for more than half of all fortunes over $1 million during the postwar period. In 1982, half of the members of the *Forbes* 400 inherited their wealth, while many of the rest made their money from oil, timber, real estate, or other commodities that had benefited from years of high inflation. In that same year, there were only thirteen billionaires in America, compared to more than four hundred today.

The postwar years were so egalitarian that economists would later label them "the Great Compression," since the gap between the rich and the rest actually shrank. It was also a period of anti-elitism in culture, when the rigid manners, moral code, and snobbery of old money were widely ridiculed. The rich were embarrassed to flaunt their wealth, or what little of it they had left after paying taxes (the top marginal tax rate was 90 percent after the war). Plus the family trusts had to be divided among squabbling heirs in Palm Beach, Newport, and Greenwich. *Science Digest* observed in 1948: "The old habits of smoking cigars wrapped in hundred-dollar bills, throwing banquets for dogs or giving $50,000 parties with automobiles as door prizes are out."

During the culture wars of the 1960s, this reverse snobbery took on added intensity as the wealthy came under fire from the egalitarian, anti-establishment.

An article in the *New York Times* in 1982 quotes a defensive Rose Sachs, a commercial real estate baroness, saying the image of the leisure class as all leisure was insulting. "We have this terrible image that we play all the time," she told the *Times*. "I went to three balls last night, and all of them were for charity."

Nineteen eighty-two, however, would set the stage for an unprecedented party of wealth.

Throughout American history, large wealth booms have been created by the convergence of three forces: deregulation and pro-wealth government policies, technological innovation, and financial speculation. In 1982, the personal computer was the big emerging technology. *Time* magazine in 1982 named the computer its Man of the Year, noting that the growing popularity of the PC heralded a new age of bits and bytes. In 1980, companies such as IBM, Hewlett-Packard, and Apple sold 724,000 personal computers. By 1982, the number had more than quadrupled.

Time noted that "the enduring American love affairs with the automobile and the television set are now being transformed into a giddy passion for the personal computer. This passion is partly fad, partly a sense of how life could be made better, partly a gigantic sales campaign. Above all, it is the end result of a technological revolution that has been in the making for four decades and is now, quite literally, hitting home."

The new technologies created massive personal wealth and allowed people and companies in almost every industry to spread their products over a wider market. As a result, the market winners had larger spoils. "The services of the best performers can be reproduced, or 'cloned,' at low additional cost," wrote Robert H. Frank and Philip J. Cook in *The Winner-Take-All Society*. "More generally, whenever there are economies of scale in production or distribution, there is a natural tendency for one product, supplier or service to dominate the market. The battle is to determine which one it will be."

Government policy also flipped in favor of the wealthy in 1982. In 1981, Ronald Reagan persuaded Congress to pass the Economic Recovery Tax Act, which lowered the top marginal tax rate from 70 to 50 percent and reduced other taxes on individuals and companies. Tax rates for non-wealthy Americans also dropped. Yet the biggest beneficiaries in dollar terms were the wealthy, who enjoyed one of the largest tax cuts in American history. In 1982, Congress passed the Garn–St. Germain Depository Institutions Act, which deregulated savings and loan associations and relaxed the constraints on home mortgages. The changes led to a surge in real estate lending and buying, and a boom in real estate values.

The Federal Reserve may have played a larger role in the wealth revolution of 1982 than either Reagan or Congress. The 1980–82 recession was widely blamed on Federal Reserve chairman Paul Volcker, whose interest-rate hikes tamed years of runaway inflation but also caused an economic crash. By the end of 1982, however, Volcker's strategy started working, and interest rates and inflation both started to fall.

The combination of lower interest rates and financial deregulation unleashed a flood of money into the financial system. The total value of the Standard and Poor's (S&P) 500 jumped from $863 million in 1981 to $1.2 trillion in 1983, adding more than $1.4 trillion in market wealth by the end of the 1980s.

As more and more companies began doling out stock as part of their executive compensation, top executives and corporate founders got a larger portion of their pay in stock. That linked more of their fortunes to the stock market and gave them a growing share of the more than $1 trillion in new market wealth during the 1980s. By 1989, the wealthiest 5 percent of Americans owned 73 percent of the individually held stocks (it is 82 percent today).

Lower interest rates also touched off a wave of deals. Debt became known as "leverage" and fueled a wave of deal making and buy-outs. In *The Snowball,* a biography of Warren Buffett, author Alice Schroeder described the period between 1982 and 1987 as a Renaissance in finance. "With debt now cheap, would-be buyers of a company could use the company's soon-to-be gutted assets as collateral to finance its purchase—like getting a hundred percent mortgage on a house," she wrote. "It cost no more to buy a huge company than to set up a lemonade stand. The merger boom had begun."

The volume of shares traded on the New York Stock Exchange more than tripled between 1980 and 1990, fueled partly by the mass of Americans who were investing their retirement money in mutual funds and stocks. By the early 1990s, profits from finance, insurance, and real estate (known as FIRE) overtook profits from manufacturing—a complete reversal from 1980, when manufacturing profits were twice as much as the profits from FIRE.

By 1986, many of the country's top one hundred earners were in finance. Michel David-Weill of Lazard Frères was making $125 million a year, while George Soros, who ran an exotic new form of financial vehicle called a hedge fund, made more than

$90 million. Michael Milken, who had yet to be implicated in an insider-trading scandal, was making nearly $80 million.

It wasn't just pure financiers who benefited from this new gusher of wealth. In addition to corporate executives, who were increasingly paid in stock and options, entrepreneurs and business owners cashed in by taking their companies public or selling them to competitors. There have always been entrepreneurs and privately owned companies in America. Yet the 1980s gave them a chance to trade in their respectable annual profits for one giant payday.

In addition to unleashing a gusher of financial wealth, 1982 also introduced a new era of asset bubbles. The amount of cash sloshing around the world swelled from retirement accounts, governments, and companies looking for short-term gains. Technology allowed investors to move billions with the click of a button, creating sudden capital stampedes.

Jeremy Grantham, the financial market guru who helps manage more than $100 billion in assets, has studied hundreds of asset bubbles over history and says that the past thirty years in America stand out for their frothiness.

"If you look at financial bubbles and financial markets, you see that the period until the 1970s was very flat, very boring, and then it steadily began to increase at an accelerating rate."

The bubbles that preceded the dot-com bust of 2000 and the real estate and then the financial crisis of 2008 marked a new level in bubbliness, he says, and even bigger ones are on the way.

"It looks like maybe we're heading in to what you might call a paradigm jump from 2007 onwards, into a period of a lot of bubbly activity, much more than normal," he told me. "Selling all those financial services is hardly going to make the world a more stable place. Much more likely it will stir up activity. It is much better financially for Wall Street to have an unstable system than a stable system. If the S&P just grew at its long-term trend rate every year, everyone would die of boredom and the deals would dry up and it would be a different world. You wouldn't have these great leaps and crashes. It's turned into a circus, and the huge explosion in financial services since the 1980s has a lot to do with it."

Grantham argues that there is a historical connection between bubbles and wealth booms. America's largest bubble periods—the Gilded Age after the Civil War, the late 1920s, and the 2000s—also marked eras of peak wealth, suggesting that large concentrations of wealth may be both a cause and an effect of speculative frenzies.

"Speculative asset bubbles correspond to periods of highest inequality," he said. "To me they are clearly interrelated. In the 1920s, you had this colossal increase in wealth associated with stock and speculation. In 2000, you had the creation of new companies where one minute it's a gleam in someone's eye and the next minute it's worth billions of dollars.

"Wealth gets flashed around like an aphrodisiac. It encourages everyone to roll the dice and take risks and make millions."

LIFESTYLES OF THE RICH AND ANXIOUS

The aphrodisiac allure of wealth spilled into American culture, where television, movies, music, and magazines began to glorify the pursuit of wealth. After the economic doldrums of the 1970s and the recession of 1982, Americans yearned for a new national confidence and prosperity. The top network TV show in 1982 was *Dallas*, the series chronicling the oversize mansions, limos, diamonds, and family battles of the oil-rich Ewing family. The shows *Falcon Crest* and *Dynasty*, which also were popular, helped make a mass market for wealth voyeurism. The king of rich-people TV, Robin Leach and his *Lifestyles of the Rich and Famous*, followed soon after, famously wishing his audiences "champagne kisses and caviar dreams."

Nineteen eighty-two also marked the launch of the first *Forbes* 400 list of richest Americans. The list recalled the fabled "Four Hundred," the group of A-list New Yorkers from the nineteenth century. (The story goes that four hundred was the maximum number who could fit in society queen Caroline Astor's ballroom, but alas, it's just a canard.) *Forbes* magazine's founder, B. C. Forbes, published a briefer, similar list in 1918, but it didn't catch on at the time. The 1980s were ripe for such an undertaking, however. To make the 1982 list, which included thirteen American billionaires, the entrants were required to have $75 million or more (it's over $1 billion now). The richest man in America in 1982 was Daniel Ludwig, a ninety-five-year-old shipping magnate who turned a small paddle steamer into the fifth-largest tanker fleet in the United States. Yet Ludwig was more the exception than the rule. Most of those on the *Forbes* list inherited their wealth or made it from oil. Texas had sixty-five residents on the 1982 list, by far the largest state contingent in the country.

With the collapse of the old codes of wealth—family pedigree, membership clubs, pet-like names such as "Bitsy"—spending became the new status marker. *U.S. News and World Report* declared, "Wealth is back in style. The old less-is-more, down-with-materialism atmosphere that achieved a high-art patina during the Carter years has been brushed aside by the new ruling class. A flaunt-it-if-you-have-it style is rippling in concentric circles across the land."

The changes in government and the economy, combined with a wealth-cheering culture, reinvigorated the wealth divide in America. After seeing their share of national wealth decline since the Great Depression, the top 1 percent saw their share of both income and wealth suddenly start to rise. In 1981, the top 1 percent had 8 percent of the nation's income; by 1990, they held 13 percent. In 1981, there were about 638,000 millionaires in America; by 1985, there were more than 800,000.

To see this transformation of the American rich from moderately wealthy makers of things to otherworldly rich beneficiaries of financial markets, consider the story of the Stern family.

THE GOLDEN CANARIES

In 1926, Max Stern, a young textile manufacturer in Germany, was nearly broke. Germany was suffering from hyperinflation and high unemployment. When the Stern family's textile business closed, twenty-eight-year-old Max went looking for work.

He wanted to go to America, but he had no cash. When a childhood friend offered to repay a loan from Max with five thousand singing canaries, Max accepted. He boarded a steamship of the Hamburg American line bound for New York, getting a ticket in exchange for paying the freight charges on the canaries. He spent much of the journey in the cargo hold, feeding and caring for the birds.

Max arrived in a New York that was booming from Wall Street profits and the growth in autos and railroads. Max didn't speak English and didn't have any friends or relatives in the city. But within days, he sold all of canaries to the John Wanamaker department store in Manhattan. Max Stern, textile manager, was now in the bird business.

He set up an office in lower Manhattan and started traveling back and forth to Germany to bring back more birds. He sold them to R. H. Macy's, Sears Roebuck, F. W. Woolworth, and other stores. By 1932, Max was the nation's largest livestock importer.

Since the customers who bought birds needed something to feed them, Max started selling bird seed. He created a new brand, called Hartz Mountain, named after one of his favorite mountain regions in Germany.

In 1959, Max's twenty-one-year-old son, Leonard, took over the business. Leonard loved selling, and as a boy had done door-to-door sales. He graduated from New York University's School of Commerce and earned his MBA while working as a clerk.

After joining his dad, Leonard expanded the business into other kinds of pet products, from Hartz Dog Pretzels (and their puppy version, called Pup-zels) to parakeet training recordings and rawhide bones. By the 1960s, Hartz flea collars, pet sham-poos, and cat litters were also top sellers.

The pet food business was hugely successful. Industry pundits claimed that Max and Leonard Stern had done for pet supplies what Henry Ford had done for the auto industry. By the 1960s, the Stern family was doing so well that they had excess cash. Leonard looked around for a new business that could soak up capital but would require far fewer workers than the pet food business, which employed thousands.

"I wanted to find something that I could run that could han-dle more capital without creating a big organization," he told me. He explored the Manhattan real estate market but decided it was already saturated. Leonard wanted to build his own venture from the ground up. While exploring the outskirts of New York City, he discovered a large plot of swampland and defunct pig farms in the New Jersey Meadowlands, six miles from downtown Manhat-tan. He bought more than twelve hundred acres and began devel-oping warehouses and offices.

As Leonard's fortunes grew from real estate and dog chews, his family also grew. Leonard's two sons, Edward and Emanuel, began to work their way up the corporate ladder, and in the 1990s Emanuel started running the real estate division, while Edward took over the pet business.

By the end of the 1990s, the pet business had become less attractive. Hartz had gotten hit with a spate of antitrust lawsuits, claiming the company was strong-arming distributors and retailers into shutting out competitors. The suits were settled, and while Hartz never admitted to wrongdoing, it had to pay a $20,000 fine to the Federal Trade Commission.

The consumer landscape was also becoming less friendly. As retailers shifted from mom-and-pop stores to giant big-box retailers and nationwide drug chains, they had more leverage to drive down Hartz's prices.

"We went from, like, forty-five-hundred customers down to about twenty," he said. "That's not a good prescription for large profits. But there was also a human element to it. Before, you would do all this product development and bring a great new product to the customer, and they would be very appreciative. But it changed and just became about data rather than personal touch. You'd bring in a new product and before you left it was being copied in Japan or China."

The biggest problem was the family. Edward "Eddie" Stern grew up with a view of wealth that was different from his father's and grandfather's. For him, the best path to wealth was finance, not bird food or buildings. Eddie saw that in a world of fast-moving global capital, you didn't have to make anything tangible to get rich. You merely had to make good bets—preferably with other people's money.

"When I grew up," Leonard said, "the kids I knew who had money had private family businesses. One kid's parents owned a thirty-store drugstore chain; another kid's family made picture frames; another kid's family made suits. Those kinds of family businesses don't exist anymore. For my son, for people now in their thirties and forties, they saw a whole different kind of wealth. He grew up, you know, where one friend's dad was a partner at Goldman Sachs and another's dad was at Credit Suisse. That's where the money is now. That's the opportunity. And, frankly, I don't blame them. It becomes seductive when a college grad can get into one of these financial companies and make $300,000 a year."

Eddie, in other words, wanted to join the ranks of those who make money from money. Leonard, by contrast, has a visceral dislike for bankers and Wall Street.

"I don't invest in the stock market," he says. "I dislike the stock market. I dislike bankers. I've always said, 'There are people who grow tomatoes and people who trade them.' For me, I like to grow the tomatoes."

After some heated internal debate, according to family friends, the Sterns sold the pet business in 2000. Eddie devoted his time to managing the family's investment portfolio, which grew by over $100 million after the pet business sale.

Eddie had already been trading on a small scale since 1998. But in 2000 he established a full-fledged hedge fund, called Canary Capital Partners, along with its management company, Canary Investment Management (named for the German birds that started it all). He also started taking in money from outside investors.

In two years, he had $400 million under management—more than the entire value of the pet business his family had built over two generations. In 2002, his assets grew to $730 million. He earned impressive returns. In 2000, when the S&P 500 fell 9 percent, Canary posted returns of nearly 50 percent. The next year, as the S&P fell further, Canary gained 29 percent.

Eddie charged his investors a fee of 1.5 percent of the funds under management as well as taking 25 percent of the profits, bringing in tens of millions a year for himself and a handful of employees. The only problem was that one of Canary's main strategies—known as "market timing," or quickly trading in and out of mutual funds—violated securities rules.

Eddie Stern faced illegal-trading charges by the New York State Attorney General in 2003. He settled the case for $40 million and, while not admitting to any wrongdoing, he agreed not to trade in mutual funds or manage any public investment funds for ten years.

Leonard, Eddie's father, now runs his own philanthropy, the Stern Foundation. He donated $30 million to New York University in 1988 to help expand the business school, which was renamed the Leonard N. Stern School of Business. When I asked whether this new form of financial wealth—often revered by Stern students anxious to start work on Wall Street—is good or bad for the economy, Leonard paused before responding. "I can't answer that question. In my generation, my peer group, we felt that to be entrepreneurs and to achieve the American dream, we had to make things. The next generation grew up incorporating different ideas of wealth and success. They start with the idea of a transaction."

SEPARATION ANXIETY

The Sterns have so far managed the move to transactional wealth without any major blowups, except for their brief run-in with the law. Yet by shifting their fortune from dog collars and bird seed to leveraged real estate and financial markets, the family is no longer rooted in the mass consumer market or broad economic growth. They are tied to asset bubbles, stocks, and fast-moving money flows.

The Sterns are part of what economists have called "The Great Financialization"—the long-term rotation of the American economy from production to finance. The moves have led to a host of changes in the broader economy, lending credence to John Maynard Keynes's fear that speculation would one day dominate over production. Many economists argue that financialization has created rising personal debts, a surge in complex financial products, and more powerful and frequent financial bubbles. It has also generated vast amounts of wealth for entrepreneurs and investors like the Sterns.

That wealth, however, has come with a price. Today's fortunes are more abstracted from the real world and therefore less stable. While the wealthy will earn far more during booms, they will also be far more vulnerable to busts as they ride the increasingly violent waves of finance. Pet food sales don't suddenly fall off a cliff. Financial markets, however, can suddenly crash due to elusive factors like "confidence" and "sentiment."

Stocks and financial markets can be twenty times more volatile than the broader economy. Because the fates of so many of today's rich are linked to those markets, the wealthy have also become more manic. Their pre-1982 financial patterns, where they gained less than the population during booms and lost more during busts, have been reversed. During all of the expansions of the past thirty years, the top earners have gained far more than the population. During the expansion of 1982 and 1989, the incomes of the top 1 percent grew by 8 percent—four times the growth of the rest of the population. The disparity was repeated during growth spurts in the late 1990s and mid-2000s.

On the way down, the biggest earners are also the biggest losers. In the recession of 1989–1991, the top 1 percent saw their incomes drop an average of 3.5 percent, compared to 1.7 percent for all Americans. In the 2000–2003 downturn, rich incomes fell 5.8

percent, compared to 2.3 percent nationally, and in 2007–2008, their incomes fell 8.4 percent compared to 2.6 percent for the country. The incomes of the top-earning four hundred Americans fell four times as much as the rest of the population's. Between 2007 and 2009, the number of Americans earning $1 million or more a year dropped by a staggering 40 percent, according to the IRS. With each economic cycle, the gains and losses of the rich became greater.

DEFINING BETA

These gains and losses can be measured by their "beta." Beta, the second letter of the Greek alphabet, is perhaps better known as a reference to a software prototype or a physics particle. In the world of statistics and finance, however, it refers to relative volatility. *Merriam-Webster* defines "beta" as "a measure of the risk potential of an investment portfolio expressed as a ratio of the stock's or portfolio's volatility to the volatility of the market as a whole."

Put another way, beta measures how much something moves compared to its peers. A beta of 1.0 indicates that the stock (or whatever is being measured) closely follows the movements of the overall market. A beta of more than 1.0 means the stock swings higher or lower than the rest of the market. For instance, the stock of Wynn Casinos, the Las Vegas gambling company, is one of the most volatile stocks in the S&P 500 and has a beta of 1.7, due to the fickle nature of gambling profits. Companies like General Mills and Kellogg's have a beta of .45, since their profits and stock movements are fairly constant.

The earnings beta of the rich makes gambling stocks look downright safe by comparison. In their groundbreaking study of high incomes, economists Jonathan Parker and Annette Vissing-Jorgensen found that the beta of the top 1 percent of earners before 1982 was lower than 1.0, meaning the volatility of their incomes was lower than that of the rest of the population. After 1982, their beta soared to an astounding 2.0. For the super-earners, or the top .01 percent, the beta jumped to more than 3.0, making the earnings of the super-rich even more volatile than the most speculative stocks on Wall Street. This is hard to believe, of course, especially in our age of ever-growing wealth and income disparities. Every day we see headlines about the rich getting ever richer and grabbing more and more of the national wealth. This is true, to some extent. As we noted earlier, the top 1 percent of earners now earn 22 percent of the nation's income, up from 9 percent in 1982. We hear about CEOs and Wall Street bankers getting multimillion-dollar bonuses even if they destroy shareholder value and rely on bailouts from the taxpayers.

Yet CEOs have actually seen their pay become less stable. A study of pay for all the CEOs of S&P 500 companies (which include the vast majority of the highest-paid corporate chiefs) found that their average income has become far more volatile since the 1980s. It more than quadrupled during the 1990s before falling by 50 percent in the early 2000s. It then jumped 50 percent and fell by half again in the late 2000s, according to the study by Steven N. Kaplan of the University of Chicago Booth School of Business.

These CEOs still make huge money, an average of $8 million each—when they have a job. But turnover has soared along with competition, leaving half of the low-performing CEOs out of work within five years.

As for the Wall Street bankers, they remain a small minority in Richistan, even if they make a lot of headlines. One of the most detailed studies to date on the occupations of the top earners, by Jon Bakija, Adam Cole, and Bradley T. Heim, found that financial professionals (which also includes those who work in the insurance industry) accounted for only 18 percent of the top 1 percent of earners. The largest category was executives, managers, and supervisors—with many or most of that group being owners of privately held businesses.

Some might argue that the money swings of the rich are voluntary, since they can manage their incomes through their investments, especially stock sales. A rich investor, for instance, might decide to sell $20 million in stock one year but none the next. He might be selling because he's buying a house, or because he thinks markets will go down, or because taxes might be going up. The investor's income appears to change dramatically. But the change doesn't reflect hardship or any change in lifestyle.

Yet even without these voluntary factors and stock sales, the incomes and wealth of the rich have become far more volatile. The Parker and Vissing-Jorgensen study stripped out stock sales, transfers, taxes, and capital gains and found that the incomes of the rich "moved substantially more (in percentage terms) than the overall average in each boom and recession since 1982." They added that "prior to 1982, this was not the case."

It's not just their incomes that have become wobbly. It's also their total net worth, or accumulated wealth. The median wealth of the American population fell by 3 percent during the 1990 recession, while the median wealth for the richest 20 percent of American fell three times as much. In the 2001–2002 recession, the top 20 percent lost three times as much of their wealth as the rest of America. Federal Reserve economists noted that during the 1990 and 2001 recessions, "only households in the highest quintile [top 20 percent] experienced significant decreases in mean and median wealth." The top 20 percent were also the biggest wealth losers during the beginning of the 2007 recession.

Between 2008 and 2010, millionaire investors lost between 20 percent and 30 percent of their net worth, one of the largest losses among the rich since the early 1930s. Nearly a fifth of millionaire investors lost nearly half of their fortunes.

Wealth in America, of course, has always been transient: As an anonymous banker wrote in 1932, "So often have I seen the most solid and respected fortunes swept away, so often have I watched the cycle from shirt sleeves to shirt sleeves, that I am inclined to regard money riches as a restless visitor who seldom sits down."

Yet wealth is now more restless than ever—even during good times. A Census Bureau study shows that from 2004 to 2007, about a third of the households in the highest income quintile moved down to another income group. In the same period, a third of those in the lowest income group moved to a higher group.

At the very top, the losses during downturns can be staggering. Sheldon Adelson, the Las Vegas casino king, lost more than $25 billion (or more than 80 percent of his net worth) during the Great Recession as his company's stock crashed. His losses worked out to $65 million a day (or $2.7 million an hour) during 2008, topping the *Forbes* list of biggest losers. Adelson and twenty-five other billionaires lost a combined $167 billion in eleven months, as their shares fell an average of 59 percent.

Adelson took the paper losses in stride—as he should have, since he was still a billionaire after the drop and would quickly recover most of his wealth within the next two years. "So I lost $25 billion," Adelson told ABC News. "I started out with zero. There is "no such thing as fear—not to an entrepreneur. Concern, yes. Fear, no."

Yet several CEOs of big companies were publicly embarrassed in 2008 and 2009 by margin calls from banks that lent them money against their company stock. The executives were essentially borrowing against their shares to make other investments or purchases. When the stocks tanked, they had to pay the loan back or sell shares.

Bruce Smith, the former CEO of Tesoro Corp., an oil refiner based in San Antonio, was forced to sell 251,100 shares, or 14 percent of his holdings in the company, to meet a margin call from Goldman Sachs Group. The co-founders of medical equipment maker Boston Scientific Corp. were forced to sell 31 million shares, which had been pledged to collateralize a loan, the company said. The CEO of Williams-Sonoma Inc. reported the sale of $13 million in company stock, also due to a margin call.

Chesapeake Energy CEO Aubrey K. McClendon had to unload almost all of his stake in Chesapeake because of a margin call. Bankers who saw McClendon's portfolio said he had pledged many of his shares for loans that he then used to leverage and invest in private equity and other investments—essentially piling risk upon risk. He later auctioned off thousands of bottles of wine from his collection to raise capital, though a spokesman for McClendon insisted he simply wanted to trim his collection.

The losers included not only Wall Street bankers and executives with stock options but also the legions of entrepreneurs and family business owners who cashed in on the asset bubbles and market booms by selling their companies. We'll explore the most radical wealth blowups in the second part of the book. But to understand the day-to-day risks of turning a business fortune into a financial one—a widespread phenomenon among the wealthy over the past thirty years—consider the story of the Maher family.

THE CULT OF LIQUIDITY

In 1945, a young American soldier named Michael Edward Maher left behind the battlefields of France and sailed to New York to rebuild his life. He had grown up in Manhattan's Hell's Kitchen, the son of poor Irish immigrants. His father worked as a longshoreman, and his mother died when he was young. As a boy, Michael knew only one kind of work: loading cargo on the docks of Manhattan. He spent summers working alongside his father on Manhattan's Chelsea Piers, and later he worked on the docks to put himself through law school. He got a law degree from St. John's University and set up his own practice in Queens, hoping to finally escape the backbreaking drudgery, the union thugs, and the corruption of cargo work.

When he enlisted in the army in 1942, he hoped to work in the Judge Advocate General's Corps. The army said it had too many lawyers, but it was suffering from a shortage of shipping experts. When they learned Michael had experience as a longshoreman, they placed him in the Transportation Corps.

He was sent off to Le Havre, France, where he helped oversee the supply chain for military campaigns in Africa and Europe. When the war ended, Michael planned to return to his law practice. But a colonel from the army who had a barge business in New York harbor convinced him to return to the docks. Michael bought up surplus army cranes and other shipping equipment and began renting them out to stevedoring companies.

He won a few contracts with shipping companies and eventually built a successful small business. His efforts to expand, however, were blocked by the tight ring of unions, organized crime families, corrupt politicians, and entrenched stevedoring companies that had a lock on the New York waterfront. Maher decided to venture farther south in search of more welcoming shores.

In 1951, he set up shop in Port Newark, in the tidal wetlands of New Jersey's Newark Bay. He started buying cranes and equipment and formed Maher Terminals to load and unload ships pulling into the port. Later he moved to nearby Port Elizabeth, an old swamp that had been filled in and developed by the Port Authority of New York and New Jersey.

The unions in Port Elizabeth were far more hospitable, since they were desperate for work. As the major New York ports became overcrowded and priced out of the market, Maher's terminal in Port Elizabeth started getting the overflow. Maher's inability to break into the secret society of the New York cargo docks proved to be his greatest stroke of luck.

His success, however, came from more than just being at the right place at the right time. Michael Maher made two big business bets that would eventually wipe out his competitors and create one of the country's largest shipping fortunes.

In the mid-1950s, Port Newark served as the launchpad for one of the world's first shipping containers—the giant, uniform metal boxes that could be loaded onto trains, planes, and trucks. While many cargo terminal operators saw containers as a costly fad that would never catch on, Maher saw them as the future. He became one of the first in the country to convert his port operations to containers. Port Elizabeth also had far better access to interstate highways, railroads, and airports than New York, making it an ideal container hub. As containers became the building blocks of global trade, Maher's terminal flourished.

He was also was an early adopter of computers. He hired a team of young programmers in the 1970s to design one of the first systems to track and manage cargo, and Port Newark's terminals became some of most technologically advanced in the country. In 1985, thanks in large part to Michael Maher, Port Elizabeth became the largest port in the world as measured by volume.

In his personal life, Michael remained a modest man. He invested most of his profits back into the company and lived with his wife and five children in a three-story colonial house in Short Hills, New Jersey. He carried a beat-up leather briefcase and drove Volvos that had been damaged during shipping and were sold for a discount. "His life was the business," says Joe Curto, president of Maher Terminals and a longtime employee. "He was on the docks at night, weekends, whatever it took."

Michael's two sons, Basil and Brian, grew up working alongside their father as forklift mechanics or messengers. Basil said some of his earliest memories were of the mountains of rubber, steel, and fragrant coffee piled high in the terminal warehouses. The boys later worked in the corporate office learning the finances and management of the business.

In the 1980s, Michael began to gradually hand over control of the business to his sons, especially to Brian. Michael remained chairman until the day he died in 1995. Basil and Brian followed their father's path of innovation and opened up a new terminal in Prince Rupert, British Columbia, which they saw as a new Port Elizabeth. They had plans to pass the business to their own children and continue to grow beyond the shores of the United States.

Like their father, the Maher brothers saw their life as their work. They both lived in New Jersey, and on their rare days off they liked to golf or go trout fishing. "All we ever knew was the shipping business," said Basil, a soft-spoken man with a weathered face and starched white dress shirts. "It's in our blood."

By the mid-2000s, however, a new era was dawning in the shipping business. Overseas giants such as Dubai Ports World, with backing from their governments, were swallowing up ports around the globe and consolidating their power. The Mahers worried about their ability to compete and raise capital. They never liked debt. And they were stunned by the huge prices that Dubai and others were willing to pay for operations such as theirs.

So in 2007, Basil and Brian and their families decided to sell Maher Terminals to an investment unit of Deutsche Bank. The price: more than $1 billion. The sale was the culmination of three generations of work and planning by the Maher family. For more than fifty years they had outsmarted and outfought unions, organized crime, Greek shipping dynasties, Korean cartels, and fast-changing global trade patterns to preserve their business. Now that they had finally achieved what the rich call a "liquidity event"—a sudden windfall from the sale of a company—they assumed their toughest business fights were behind them. They could spend the rest of their lives relaxing, playing golf, supporting charities, and spending time with their families.

While the Mahers could overcome even the toughest union bosses and organized crime families, they were no match for the Wall Street firms that promised to help them manage their new-found fortune.

Michael Maher had always told his sons to avoid Wall Street and avoid buying stocks. "He would tell us, 'I was poor once. I don't ever want to be poor again,'" recalled Brian.

Michael invested only in municipal bonds, both for himself and for the company pension fund. His sons followed his lead—for the most part. Basil made a brief foray into stock picking in the 1980s but quit after losing $1,000. "That was a lot for me at the time," he said.

When they sold their business, the Mahers knew that they couldn't trust themselves with their windfall. They were shipping guys, not investors. They wanted to park their cash in a safe place until they could hire their own staff of well-trained investors and create a long-term plan that included their charities, kids, and estates.

They deposited their money in three different banks—Lehman Brothers, UBS, and JPMorgan Chase—so that they could spread the risks. On the advice of a Wall Street friend, the Mahers sent the banks written investment guidelines with one chief goal: to preserve capital.

The accounts were "discretionary," meaning the banks could invest the money as they pleased, as long as they followed the chief goal. In addition to preserving capital, the Mahers stated that they wanted the money to be highly liquid and easily accessible if they ever wanted to withdraw it. Basically, they were asking for a savings account with a slightly better interest rate.

UBS and JPMorgan Chase put the money into U.S. Treasuries, money-market funds, and government bonds, which were all among the most conservative investments. Lehman, which received $600 million of the Mahers' money, was more creative.

When the Mahers saw their first account statement from Lehman, it showed that $400 million of their money had been invested in securities with mysterious names such as Tortoise TYY I and INC 2003–2. The Mahers called a friend who worked on Wall Street, and the friend called Lehman and asked, "What's this 'Tortoise' doing in the Mahers' portfolio?" Lehman explained that the investments were auction-rate securities—a kind of short-term bond that Wall Street had introduced in the late 1980s. Bankers had been telling investors for years that auction-rate securities were "cash equivalents," meaning they were just as safe as cash.

The problem with auction-rate securities—a problem that bankers usually failed to explain—is that they trade in an obscure and largely opaque Dutch auction market. Every week or every month, depending on the security, an auction-rate security comes up for sale at an auction and has its interest rate reset. For more than twenty years, the auctions had gone smoothly. Then in 2008, just when the Mahers discovered they had $400 million in auction-rate securities, the auctions started failing, meaning their $400 million was frozen and impossible to value. Their goals of preserving capital and maintaining liquidity had been shattered.

Through their Wall Street intermediary, the Mahers instructed Lehman to sell their auction rates. Lehman was able to sell about $114 million of their holdings. Before they could dump the rest, the auction market seized up because there were no buyers. In early 2008, the subprime mortgage crisis was beginning to turn into a full-blown credit crisis, which left auction-rate securities stranded and the Mahers with $286 million of worthless paper. They filed a claim against Lehman, accusing the company of mishandling their investments.

Lehman would later go bankrupt itself, due in part to its own holdings of poorly understood debt products. Yet before the firm failed, Lehman justified its decisions to the Mahers by saying that auction-rate securities had always been as safe as cash. They added that since their account was discretionary, the brothers had agreed to allow Lehman to make the investment decisions. They said the Mahers' investment statement expressly allowed for auction-rate securities and other "cash equivalents" and that the Mahers were just looking for someone to blame for a broader financial crisis.

The Mahers still had plenty of money—hundreds of millions, in fact—even if they assumed their $286 million was gone for good. They could fund charities, set up trusts for grandkids, and pay for as many golf games and trout-fishing trips as they wanted. Yet the loss still stung. "I don't care who you are—$286 million is a lot of money," Brian said.

The Mahers hated public attention, and until I talked to them in 2008—after repeated phone calls, written requests, and discussions with their attorney—they had never given an interview to the mainstream press. Filing a lawsuit was a painful act of highly visible protest. What the Mahers really wanted was for Lehman to admit wrongdoing. It wasn't just about the money. It was about the principle of a Wall Street firm squandering years of hard work by the Maher family. It was about holding Wall Street accountable.

"We entrusted our money to Lehman believing them to be looking out for our best interests," Brian said. "They didn't."

Even though they lost $180 million, the Mahers got off rather lightly relative to their overall fortune. Other rich people weren't so lucky. While some investors and Wall Streeters recovered quickly from the recession, the American rich who rode the asset bubbles and lending booms of the past two decades have done far worse.

PART II

---•---

The Suddenly Non-Rich

3

HOMES LIKE

WHITE ELEPHANTS

Jackie Siegel is pacing the floor of her future 7,200-square-foot ballroom. The former beauty queen, with platinum-blond hair, blue eye shadow, and a white minidress, clacks along the plywood construction boards in her high heels trailed by a small entourage of helpers and staff.

"This is the grand hall," she says, opening her arms to a space the size of a concert hall and surrounded by balconies. "It will fit five hundred people comfortably, probably more. The problem with our place now is that we when have parties with, like, four hundred people, it gets too crowded."

She moves on to a pair of giant steel staircases that spill down from the second floor. "We have two grand staircases, so when we have big events, I would come down one set of stairs and David would walk down the other. With the music playing and the lights and the crowd, it would be a really great entrance for the host couple."

She points to the ring of balconies on the second floor, over-looking the ballroom.

"That's where all the kids will be, watching and looking down at the parties at night. Or maybe David would stand in the center balcony to give his speech, and then we'd have fireworks out the front window with an orchestra. Like Disney."

For now, the Siegel dream home is still a work in progress, with its steel ribs and framing rising above the ballroom like a great dinosaur skeleton. The bones hint at a lost age of excess: there's the concrete strip for the future bowling alley, the sunken concrete tubs for the spa, relaxing pools, and massage rooms, and the giant oval for an indoor skating rink. The framing outlines the home's ten kitchens, twenty-three bathrooms, thirteen bed-rooms, two elevators, two movie theaters (one for kids and one for adults, each modeled after a French opera theater), a twenty-car garage, a wine cellar designed to hold twenty thousand bottles, and the main swimming pool (one of six) overlooking the lake.

"It really doesn't feel that big, does it?" Jackie says. "I mean, it's big, but it has the feel of a family home. It's cozy. It was the smart layout, I think."

Jackie has an equally clever solution for getting around the mansion, which at 90,000 square feet is the largest private home in America. She and her husband and eight kids will each get Seg-ways.

"My husband has a great joke—he says that once we move in, we're not going to see our kids until the day they graduate from college."

The staff will also be sequestered, in a hidden warren of bed-rooms, kitchens, and bathrooms in a private wing upstairs.

We walk out of the house onto the deck overlooking Lake Butler—a green emerald in the Butler Chain of Lakes, ringed by sycamore trees and their long gray beards of Spanish moss.

Jackie stands at the foot of a concrete slab that will become the Olympic-size pool, next to the future rock grotto with three hot tubs and an eighty-foot waterfall.

"We've put so much of our lives into this," she says. "Years and years and so much money and planning. It's really our dream."

As she looks out on the lake, her supermodel smile quickly fades and she wipes away a small tear.

"Maybe it will still work out," she says. "It always does, right?"

OVERSIZE HOME SYNDROME

If there were one symbol of the vast fortunes made, spent, and lost on the speculative bubble of real estate during the past twenty years, it would be the Siegels' 90,000-square-foot fantasy, called "Versailles." Versailles—or "Versize," as the Siegels pronounce it—sits on a spit of land in Isleworth, a gated community of lakeside mansions just outside Orlando, Florida. Tiger Woods's house—and his famously dented fire hydrant—is just around the corner, along with homes for other famous athletes, entertainers, and CEOs. (The Siegels' neighbor at Isleworth is a member of the rock band Coldplay.)

Isleworth and other suburbs of Orlando were flooded with money during the real estate boom, and Versailles was to be its grandest statement—twice the size of the White House, filled with antiques and chandeliers from the Old World. The Siegels poured more than $50 million into the land and construction, hoping to move in by 2011 with their eight kids, six nannies, and four dogs.

Yet today Versailles sits empty. Construction has been halted for nearly a year, and the home's ownership remains in doubt. The reason: The Siegels ran out of money. Like the original Versailles, whose enormous costs strained the finances of Louis XIV and the French economy in the 1680s, the Siegel palace stands as a monument to the family's market-fueled debt binge and spending spree of the past decade, not to mention the mega-mansion craze that gripped America's rich in the 2000s.

Versailles is on the market for $75 million as is. Buyers can get the finished version, built to the Siegels' specifications, for $100 million. As of mid-2011, the home had been on the market for over a year, with a few lowball offers but no sign of a deal. The Siegels' real estate agent, Lorraine Barrett, remained hopeful, saying she'd had a growing number of "nibbles" from Russian oligarchs and royal families in the Middle East who want to use the home as a base for their regular visits to Disney World.

"There aren't any other homes in America like this," she said, stepping over some mysterious animal droppings inside the house. "It's one of a kind."

Actually, there's a glut of unsold, unwanted mansions in America. The number of homes larger than 5,000 square feet built each year soared to more than thirty-five thousand by the late 2000s—five times the number in 1995. When the high-beta rich saw their salaries and fortunes plummet, their homes became white elephants. Some owners sold at steep discounts; others defaulted on their loans or handed them over to the lenders. A real estate bust that began with lower-income buyers and subprime mortgages reached a sector of the market that many housing economists said was immune: multimillion-dollar mansions. As we will see in other markets later in the book, the most expensive part of the housing economy, one that used to be among the most stable, has suddenly become the most volatile.

Greenwich, Connecticut, the hedge fund capital and one of the richest towns in America, still had an oversupply of multimillion-dollar mansions in 2011, long after Wall Street and hedge funds had recovered. In 2011, its supply of homes priced at $10 million would take more than three years to sell off—provided that no more homes came on the market. The town's monthly supply of cheaper homes was far smaller. In Las Vegas, more than a quarter of the mansions priced at $3 million or more were sold through foreclosure or at a loss.

In 2007, at the peak of the housing boom, the richest 1 percent of Americans held more than $3.5 trillion in residential real estate, or about 34 percent of the nation's total. The share of their fortunes devoted to real estate jumped by more than 50 percent between 1989 and 2007. Many of their real estate dreams were funded by debt. The mortgage and housing debts of the richest 1 percent of Americans more than quadrupled between 1989 and 2007, to $500 billion. Their pace of borrowing far exceeded that of the rest of the country, suggesting that it wasn't just the middle class and the poor who lived in homes beyond their means.

For many rich people, filling their McPalaces became an exercise in expansionist living. A Russian billionaire in Greenwich, Connecticut, proposed a 30,000-square-foot mansion that had twenty-six toilets. (As one commenter on my blog wrote: "What will happen if he has twenty-seven guests and they all need to go at the same time? How embarrassing.") The billionaire scaled back to fifteen toilets to appease the local zoning board.

By the late 2000s, it was not uncommon for the wealthy to have four or five residences—one or two in major cities where their businesses were based, one on the beach, one in the mountains, and one or two overseas.

In 2005, an entrepreneur named Dru Schmitt sold his St. Louis–based medical data company for $260 million and promptly ordered up a 23,000-square-foot mansion in Boca Raton. The French-country-style manor on the beach has four kinds of rare onyx in the bedroom, music piped underwater in the resort-style pool, a computerized television system holding 850 movies, and hand-shaved walnut floors. The doorknobs and hinges alone cost $160,000.

Yet after the home was finished, he discovered a problem. "When they moved in, they felt it was just too large for what they were comfortable with," Gerard Liguori, the home's broker, told me. They listed the house for $24.9 million and sold it for half that amount.

Stanley and Dorothea Cheslock built a 26,000-square-foot home in Connecticut, boasting the same beam structure found in Westminster Abbey and an elevator that looks like a giant French birdcage. The home's movie theater has its own marquee and concession stand.

The Cheslocks spent four years and $21 million building the home, which they named Hillcrest. Shortly after moving in, they put it on the market.

"It's like a Cinderella house," Dorothy Cheslock said. "To me, it's a castle. I never really needed the castle, and I think somebody else could enjoy it now." She adds, "I'm just going to go, I think, to a smaller home. But I'll take my prince with me."

"Houses, cars, investments. That's fleeting," Stanley Cheslock said. "It's really the other things that are important . . . friends and family."

The fact that Cheslock's merchant banking business lost $100 million in 2008 during the financial meltdown may have also played a role. The Cheslocks listed the home for $19 million, but as of late 2010, there were no takers.

Of all the high-beta real estate follies, however, Florida's Versailles is king. And the story of the Siegels illustrates how the rich have become both the leading beneficiaries and the most spectacular losers of the latest financial bubble.

THE MYSTERY FUN HOUSE

David Siegel is sitting in his living room, nursing a Diet Coke and petting his Great Pyrenees dog ("They were big with the French royals," he says). At seventy-eight, with slicked-back gray hair and a Hawaiian shirt and shorts, he has the look of an aging tropical tycoon, a man who has had more than his share of hard-won success and well-funded indulgence.

It's a Sunday afternoon at the Siegels' house. Their home is a 26,000-square-foot white and gold mansion named "Gull's Landing" that's filled with oversize portraits of the Siegels. There are pictures of Jackie and David with Sylvester Stallone, Jeb Bush, and Bruce Willis, and a blown-up cover of *Pageantry* magazine with Jackie on the cover and the headline "Celebrating the Glamorous Lifestyle."

The six kids are in their rooms with the nannies. Jackie wears a neon bikini top and fishnets as she hosts a barbecue party for several girlfriends. Thunderstorms have rained out the outdoor grilling, so they have the party in the kitchen instead. The song "Rich Girl" blares from the house speakers, and the women belt out the lyrics: "You can rely on the old man's money / You can rely on your old man's money."

David, oblivious to the musical ironies in the background, rubs his eyes and forehead after a long morning with lawyers and lenders. "This has been the toughest thing I've ever faced," he says. "My business has been through oil embargos, the 9/11 terrorist attacks, recessions, 21 percent interest rates, and Gulf wars. Through it all, the business never stopped growing, 20 percent a year. But this one, this is different. The one thing we cannot combat is when the financing freezes up."

To find out how the Siegels got so squeezed, and how they became models of high-beta wealth, it helps to take a trip back to
their past—to a TV repairman in Miami, and to a model from
upstate New York who vowed to one day meet a billionaire.

When he was four years old, David Siegel started a paper route,
pulling a wagon along his suburban street at dawn. "I didn't know
that you're not supposed to work at four years old," he said. "I've
been working ever since."

As he grew up, he started working in the family's grocery store,
stocking shelves, stamping prices, and working the cash register.
By the time he was ten, he said, he was managing the store when
his parents were away.

When his father sold the store and went into the furniture business, David and his brother went around the neighborhood (one
of Miami's poorest) to make deliveries and collections. After that,
he drifted from career to career. He tried going to Hollywood to
become an actor, but he said agents told him he looked too much
like Rock Hudson. He became a deputy sheriff in Florida and slept
in his squad car to save cash. He briefly considered going to Alaska.

During a visit to Mexico to see a girlfriend, David set his first—
and, he says, only—financial goal. "I decided that all I ever needed
in life was $50,000. I loved Mexico, and when I was there, people
told me I could live like a king on $5,000 a year. So I figured if I
could make $50,000, I could buy a second mortgage earning 10
percent and move to Mexico."

His dream of becoming a Mexican thousandaire never materi-
alized. On the advice of a college professor, he started taking voca-
tional classes on television and communications. His commercial
instinct quickly took over, and he and a teacher started running a
business from the school, fixing TVs. David was asked to leave the
school, since they were forbidden from using the school to operate
a business.

He set up a TV repair shop in an old dry-cleaning shop near Miami. It was a tough neighborhood, but business slowly took off. He got married and had a son. One night in 1963, when he was at the hospital to greet his second baby, he got a call from his shop. The manager had been shot and killed by a customer. Distraught over the shooting, David decided to shut the place down. He had trouble finding another job or business, however, and within six months he and his family were broke. His car was repossessed. The family was evicted from their house, and they moved to a cheap rental. That Thanksgiving, David and his wife and their two children sat in a dark kitchen with no electricity, no running water, and no food, warming a baby bottle with a candle.

"I'll never forget that day," he said. "I sat there and said to myself, 'I will never get this low again.'" The next day he went out and borrowed space to start another TV store. He bought broken TV sets from Sears and other retailers and repaired them to sell at a profit. By 1968, he was thriving again. He bought a house, got a new car, and started making plans for an even bigger store.

In the summer of 1968, riots broke out in Miami during the Republican National Convention. David got a call at 4:00 a.m. from the police, telling him his store was on fire. By the time he got there, the windows were shattered and most of the furniture was smoldering ruins. "I took one look at the store, put the car in reverse, and drove home and went to bed," he said. The next morning he told the landlord he was closing the shop.

He decided to try another line of work. Browsing the classifieds, he found an ad for a real estate salesman. He got the job and began selling Florida land to northerners. He had a knack for sales and soon signed up with another firm selling property near Orlando.

David says his wife "got tired of all the ups and downs" and became a Jehovah's Witness. They were divorced shortly after moving to Orlando.

But David's business took off as he rode the land craze sparked by Disney World and the flood of retirees heading for warmer climes. By 1975, he owned several apartment complexes, a few hotels, some gas stations, an 80-acre orange grove, and a new Cadillac. With about $3 million in the bank, he was ready to retire at the age of forty-five. "That was more money than I ever thought I'd need for the rest of my life," he says.

He invested in a new tourist attraction called the Mystery Fun House, which was styled after the old Coney Island fun houses. It quickly began minting a fortune.

One day in 1980, a developer visited David and asked to buy his orange grove. The developer said he wanted to create a time-share—a new business model at the time that allowed people to buy annual time at a property rather than the whole property.

"As soon as I heard it, I loved the idea," David said. "I kept the property and I kept the time-share idea." He started with eight units and quickly sold out. By 2010, his company, called Westgate Properties, owned twelve thousand time-share units at twenty-eight resorts in eleven states. In 2008, Westgate was on track to do $1 billion in sales. It also launched its most ambitious project ever: a $660 million, fifty-two-story Planet Hollywood tower in Las Vegas.

Of course, he had his share of controversies. The time-share business is notorious for its high-pressure sales tactics, bait-and-switch offers, and fine print. Those "free weekends in Boca" are, of course, rarely free and often end in acrimony and lawsuits. Westgate avoided the worst of the criticisms but once had to pay a $900,000 fine to the Federal Trade Commission for calling people on the national do-not-call list.

The Siegels' personal fortune expanded with the company. David never sold a single share of the company to outside investors or companies, preferring to own 100 percent himself. By the mid-2000s, the company was throwing off nearly $200 million in profits, almost all of which went into the Siegels' pockets or back into the company.

David debuted on the *Forbes* list in 2008 with an estimated net worth of $1.3 billion. "I felt invulnerable," he says. "I felt I was beyond worrying about money."

He met Jackie in 1999 at a party. She was a busty blonde former beauty queen who had just come off a divorce. And she was a woman who, as she explains, "always gets what I want." What she wants often happens to involve men with money.

She grew up in Binghamton, New York, the hard-scrabble former factory town near the Pennsylvania border. After graduating from the Rochester Institute of Technology with a degree in computer marketing, Jackie set a goal. "I was either going to go to New York and meet Donald Trump or go to the West Coast and meet Bill Gates," she says.

She decided on New York, since a friend was headed there, and within a few weeks she was dating Trump. "It was much easier than I thought," she said.

The Donald eventually moved on to Marla Maples. But Jackie— while modeling and frequently appearing on billboards—found another man. He was a wealthy Wall Streeter whose family owned an investment firm, and within weeks of meeting on the Street, they were married. During their eight-year marriage, Jackie says, she was miserable.

"He married me so his family would give him his inheritance," she says. "It wasn't a real marriage."

Jackie split her time between Florida and New York. In the midst of her divorce, she accompanied a friend to a party in

Orlando. When David walked in and saw her, he was instantly hooked.

Jackie says she didn't know about David's wealth when they started dating. But she quickly learned. After they married in 2000, they bought their 26,000-square-foot house in Isleworth. The Siegels bought a yacht and "so many cars I lost track," Jackie says. One is a stretch SUV that seats fifteen people and has eleven TV screens. They also had a small fleet of planes, including a Gulfstream III and a Pilatus.

Quantity was also a priority in their family planning. The Siegels had seven children together, and adopted an eighth. All of the kids have names that begin with *D* (as in David) or *J* (as in Jackie), and three of her sons were conceived on Labor Day and born on Memorial Day, Jackie says.

Jackie became one of Orlando's leading socialites, attending and hosting benefits, going to lunches, and flying around the country to accompany David to events and parties. To mind the house and family, she had a staff of fifteen housekeepers, six nannies, three full-time landscapers, and a full-time chef named Jeff.

They quickly outgrew their 26,000-square-foot estate. During their honeymoon in France in 2000, the couple visited Château de Versailles and toured the grounds. David asked Jackie if she liked the palace. "I said, 'Yeah, it's beautiful,'" she recalls. "So David said, 'Then I want to build a Versailles for you back in America.' Well we didn't have houses like that in Binghamton, where I grew up, so I couldn't really imagine what it would be."

Flying back in their Gulfstream, David made a sketch of their dream home on a cocktail napkin—a three-story extravaganza with multiple wings and row upon row of arched windows, porticos, and engraved royal seals. That was just the beginning.

"During the design process, the house kind of took on a life of its own," Jackie said. "I wanted a bowling alley for the kids, and I wanted an indoor skating rink. He wanted a 10,000-square-foot health spa with an indoor relaxation pool. We had to keep buying more lots of land as the house kept growing."

She says she didn't even know it was slated to be the largest home in America. One day, after construction had started, she was talking with her friend Robin Leach, the former host of *Lifestyles of the Rich and Famous*, and he told her that this Versailles would top all other private residences in the United States. (Technically, Biltmore House, built by the Vanderbilts in Asheville, North Carolina, is far larger, at 175,000 square feet. But it's now mostly a museum.)

"I was really surprised," she said. "I thought lots of people would have something bigger."

When I ask David why they decided to build such a big house, he had a simpler answer.

"Because I can."

THRIFT IS RELATIVE

In September 2008, when Lehman Brothers collapsed and financial markets fell into a swoon, the credit markets also shut down. Corporate borrowers were strapped for cash. Time-share businesses were especially hurt: not only were buyers unable to get mortgages to buy their time-shares, but banks were unwilling to lend to the time-share companies to build or expand.

Real estate had been through plenty of ups and downs over the years, though until 2008, time-shares had never had a down year since their inception in the 1960s. But in 2009, the time-share industry fell by nearly half. David's company had planned to raise $300 million in the credit markets in October 2009, but the sale was canceled. David had put $300 million of his own money into the Las Vegas project and borrowed more than $360 million. He also had debt on other properties.

All told, he figures he had more than $1 billion in debt. By 2009, with his credit lines maxed out, he slashed the company's workforce by more than half, from twelve thousand to about fifty-five hundred. And since he couldn't afford the marketing and operational costs, sales also fell by half, from $1 billion to $500 million.

Jackie and David were forced to take the first hard look at their lifestyle. During the good times, there had been few if any limits, since their cash flow came from the company. Their financial fate was intimately tied to Westgate, which seemed like a perfectly reasonable wealth-building strategy when the company was producing $200 million in profits every year.

When the economy tanked and the cycle reversed, Westgate's problems became the Siegels' problems. The banks took control of the Siegels' finances and put them on an allowance, though they decline to give the amount.

They fired fourteen of their fifteen housekeepers and let three groundskeepers go. Chef Jeff married one of the nannies and left to become a caterer. The kids were yanked from private school and put into the local public school. Jackie's personal budget was slashed, cutting short her climb through Orlando society.

David and Jackie declined to say how much money they have left, though they're still multimillionaires. Westgate has been selling properties as fast it can over the past year to pay down its debt.

Disposing of Versailles has been more difficult. They had a $10 million mortgage on the property, and after spending millions on the construction and land, they didn't have the $20 million needed to finish it. Their bank lenders grew nervous about holding such a large mortgage in one of the nation's hardest-hit housing markets. They gave the Siegels an ultimatum: either pay back the loan or sell the house—even if it was an unfinished and unsightly hunk of concrete.

"We couldn't pay it off, so we had to sell it," David says. He says he realizes now that maybe Versailles was a bad idea. Maybe, he says, he shouldn't have tried to build the largest home in America while he had $1 billion in debt. And he admits that his self-confidence, his feelings of financial invincibility, and the huge amounts of money he was making and spending may have blinded him to the risks of a fall in housing prices, lending, and credit.

"I was cocky and I didn't care what the house would cost because I couldn't spend all the money I was making. With hindsight, I should have been paying off these banks and putting money aside and having a nest egg."

As visible and tragic as Versailles may be, however, David says the house wasn't the underlying reason for his financial problems. It was just a symptom.

"I made two major mistakes," he said. "Well, I'm sure I've made a lot more than that in business, but there were two major ones. Number one, I signed personally for all the loans. I own 100 percent of the company, so when the company signed for a loan, it was me anyway. When the banks said, 'Will you personally guarantee the loan?' I'd say, 'Sure, no problem.'

"The second mistake was that I never took anything off the table. I never sold off any ownership stakes in the company. It was like a crapshooter in Vegas, and I had everything on the line."

As David sees it, the problem wasn't his spending or borrowing. His mistake was that he put too much of his own fortune at risk, rather than shifting it all to the company. "Maybe," he says, "I should have looked after myself and my family a bit more."

Today, the Siegels are trying to adapt to their more modest

lifestyle—though it's unclear how much further they will have to fall. David is scrambling to find an investor or lender to fund his business.

Jackie has started a nonprofit called ThriftMart, an enormous thrift store that accepts donated clothes and other personal items to sell them to the needy for $1 each. Many of the clothes come from Jackie's own closet. "Next week, we're having a fashion show with young girls and we're helping underprivileged children, foster children," she says. "Helping people is more important to me right now. I'm not doing it for the publicity." She adds, though, that a local news channel will be at the fashion show.

Standing in her dining room, next to a table for twenty, a glittering chandelier, and giant portraits of her and her family, Jackie says she never placed much value on material things. She says what matters to her, and what has always mattered to her, is family, friends, health, and enjoying life.

"I've learned to never take things for granted," she says. "Easy come, easy go."

The money—and loss of it—has also improved her relationship with David, she says. "It's made us stronger. Before, my husband just wanted a trophy wife, and he wanted me out there. But now things have changed, and I think he has a lot more respect for me and realizes that I do have a brain. I like the fact that I can do more and help more. Now he actually knows that I'm there for the long run and through thick and thin, up and down. He realizes that I'm still here even though we don't have a private jet anymore or a yacht."

The kids have also taken their downward mobility in stride, Jackie says. They prefer public school, she says, because they hated the uniforms and confining culture of private school. They also don't mind losing Versailles, since they were a little embarrassed by all their wealth and wanted to "fit in more with the other kids."

"They worried that if friends saw the house, they would think they're rich."

Jackie and the kids do miss one perk of their old life: the private jet. In late 2008, in the depths of the recession and anger over bank bailouts, the Siegels' lenders told them they had to give up the jets.

"One day," David said, "one of the banks came to us and said, 'How can we keep going to the government asking for money when our largest customer is flying around the country in a Gulfstream? We're sorry, but we don't want you to fly the Gulfstream anymore.'"

The Siegels had purchased the plane for about $8 million in 2003, borrowing all $8 million. Today the plane's value is about half that. Rather than write off the loan and sell the plane (or have it repo'd by Ken Cage), the Siegels are renting it out for cash.

Meantime, David and Jackie are flying commercial. Jackie's first commercial flight was to Asheville, North Carolina, where she was supposed to meet a friend in early 2010. While the plane was boarding, however, she went to the airport restroom, assuming the plane would wait. It didn't, so she took a plane to Charlotte instead and had a limousine take her to Asheville. "It was a whole fiasco," she says.

David's transition to flying commercial was even more traumatic. His first commercial flight was to Las Vegas in mid-2009. During the flight he caught a cold that he says has lasted more than a year. Flying commercial literally made him sick, he says.

"I'm probably going to have to have surgery to clean out my sinuses. All those germs on the commercial planes are terrible. I have the banks to thank for that."

For their summer vacation in 2010, the Siegels were originally going to fly across the country and stop at their favorite sites. But with their planes grounded, they were forced to take their

SUV—a few of the kids refuse to fly commercial because they are fearful of terrorist attacks, Jackie says.

The kids who have flown commercial are still getting used to the concept. Jackie and a few of the kids had recently taken a commercial flight to visit relatives. After they got on the plane and buckled themselves in, Jackie's five-year-old looked around at the other passengers and said, "Mommy, what are all these strangers doing on our plane?"

Whether the Siegels end up with $800 million or $80 million, they will still be rich by any measure. And losing the use of their Gulfstream can hardly compare with losing a home or a job, even if the Siegels consider the transition to flying commercial to be a major sacrifice.

Yet some of the high-beta rich weren't as lucky. For them, the real estate bubble, the boom in finance, and the age of free money had far more dire consequences.

4

LUCKY'S LANDING

Like the Siegels, Jack Warner built his fortune from the ground up. More precisely, he built it from the clay-packed dirt and limestone of rural Indiana.

A self-described "son of a ditchdigger," Warner started working with his father, who was an excavator, when he was ten. By the time he was fourteen, Jack was operating hydraulic excavators and driving gravel-filled dump trucks down the highway for his dad's business.

"Times were a little different back then," says Warner, a bear of a man with sparkling blue eyes, a mop of white hair, and a shaggy goatee. "People grew up faster, and nobody cared about your age or driver's licenses or anything like that. For me it was fun, being around my dad and driving trucks and operating these huge machines. It was like a boy's dream."

The fun turned into work when he was fifteen and his father left home. With no income, Jack, his mom and four siblings moved to nearby Elkhart, Indiana, where they lived in a three-room shack with no plumbing or electricity. Jack started digging trenches and working on paving crews until he could save enough money to buy his own tools and truck.

Within a year, he had his own excavation company with five employees, even though he was still in high school. He started bidding on big contracts for the state and local utilities, grading roads and sinking electrical lines. When he filled out the bidding papers, he always wrote his age down as twenty-one, even though he was fifteen. No one ever questioned him since he was huge for his age—six feet three inches tall and over 180 pounds.

Jack never liked school much. By the time he was sixteen, he had earned enough money to buy his own car. His high school cut him a deal, allowing him to miss classes and earn a diploma as long as he passed the tests, which he always did.

He got married at seventeen and had three kids. His company, Warner and Sons (even though he was the only son in the company), soon grew to sixty employees, with sales of more than $5 million a year. His annual take-home pay ballooned to more than $500,000.

For the next thirty years, Warner's life was one of hard-won success and growing comforts. He built a 6,000-square-foot home in Elkhart, with an indoor pool, Jacuzzis, a home theater, and giant flat-screen TVs. His garage expanded to house his burgeoning collection of toys, from a Corvette convertible and a Harley-Davidson to his Boss Hoss trike and trailers.

Warner has a laid-back demeanor. He's got a dark tan and usually wears shorts and T-shirts with beer logos. He's closer to the character of the Dude in *The Big Lebowski* than a steely midwestern construction magnate. His eyes and mouth are framed by deep smile lines, suggesting a life filled with laughs and playfulness.

Some days in Indiana, he and his friend Paul Shannon would

jump into Paul's plane and pick a random destination. "We'd just look at each other and say, 'Which way is the wind blowing?'" said Shannon. "We'd wind up in Florida, or Mexico, or Costa Rica, or wherever, and we had nothing but the clothes on our back, so we'd just buy a toothbrush and stay a few days."

When Jack goes to a restaurant, he never looks at the menu. He just tells the waiter or waitress, "Surprise me." He happily eats whatever is served. Jack only needs about four hours of rest a night, and he always gets up at 4:00 a.m. and works from dawn till 9:00 or 10:00 p.m.

At first Jack took his success in stride. He became something of a mud-stained patriarch in Elkhart, sponsoring Little League teams and helping out sick or financially strapped employees or friends. The highlight of his year was the annual Warner pig roast, when he would host up to five hundred people—workers, locals, friends, whoever showed up—for a two-day blowout on his property. He roasted three pigs, grilled mounds of chicken and burgers, and tapped multiple kegs of beer as guests listened to live bands he hired.

Yet as his fortune grew, Jack lost his grounding. His world, once one of constant struggle, fear, and providing for his family, became one of endless luxury and possibility. His personal life disintegrated. He got divorced from his first wife and married again, then got divorced five years later. A daughter from his first marriage died at the age of twenty-five from a rare liver disease. The other kids remained distant figures in his life, appearing only briefly in between work and parties and personal projects.

"You know, I never really got to know my kids," he says. "That's one of my biggest regrets. I was just too busy. With work. With all my side projects. With having fun, I guess."

In the 1980s, Jack became a licensed pilot and started buying planes. He worked his way up from single-engine Pipers to twin-engine Cessna 414s. He became so addicted to flying that he and some friends pooled their money and formed an airport community, called JB's Landing, where plane owners could own homes just off an airport runway for easy access.

"You could land on the runway and taxi the plane right into your garage," he says.

His favorite destinations were Florida and the Bahamas, especially during the bitter Indiana winters. The more time he spent in Florida, the more he liked it, and he decided to look for a place to retire there. His plan was to find a property on the water that could also generate income for his retirement. "I wanted something secure and stable," he said.

He scoured the Florida coast for years, working farther and farther south until he found his paradise—a run-down trailer park at the end of Little Torch Key, near the bottom of the Florida Keys.

The park was called Lucky's Landing. It had fourteen weedy acres of mobile homes, trailers, garbage, and the occasional feral dog. Jack saw potential. There were very few undeveloped properties of that size left in the lower Florida Keys, since development is so restricted. The property also had a dredged shore—unusual for the island—which was perfect for docking large boats.

Jack didn't have much experience in real estate. He was "basically just a ditchdigger with a pilot's license," he says. But Lucky's Landing seemed like a no-lose proposition. He could turn it into a condo development and sell off the plots for millions. If that didn't work, he could keep it as a trailer park and make $50,000 a month in income. Either way, it would fund a comfortable retirement.

Jack bought the property in 1993 for $1.025 million and began fixing it up with the growing cash flow from Warner and Sons. He built new boat docks, put in new roads, and added lush lawns, trees, and thousands of flowers. He built himself a 6,000-square-foot house with a resort-size pool, Jacuzzis, chef's kitchen, and seven bedrooms. By 2003, he had put more than $3.5 million into the property.

Plans for the development moved along slowly. There were partners to manage, banks to convince, and local politicians to please. But Jack was patient. He was also having the time of his life.

As a wealthy, self-employed divorcé, he reveled in the endless summer of the Florida Keys. Almost every night he went to Teasers, a strip club that featured young women from around the world. It wasn't uncommon for him to drop $200 a night at the club, mostly buying drinks for the strippers.

"It wasn't about the sex," Jack says. "They were just friends. We joked around, had fun. Some guys go to strip clubs and hit on the girls. We were all just pals."

Some of those "pals" also moved in with Jack, at least for a while. He had always been generous about letting friends or relatives stay at his houses. But Lucky's Landing became a twenty-four-hour party pad and free five-star boardinghouse. The door was never locked, and people would come and stay for days and weeks, eating his food, borrowing his cars, and sometimes leaving with his computers. The guests were almost always female and always young and attractive.

"Jack's always been a little too trusting," says his friend Paul Shannon. "Especially with pretty girls."

Warner had two rules for his house: no boyfriends and no drugs. Clothing was optional.

"I never told anyone they couldn't wear clothes," he said. "I just told them that it was their choice. So a lot of the girls who were staying at my house never wore any clothes. It's just the way life is in the Keys."

———

Indiana's attractions became less and less appealing. Warner started turning over the operations of Warner and Sons to his management. Sales and profits started to slide. At the same time, he was plowing more and more into Lucky's. He also took on a side business: manufacturing airplanes.

Jack knew as little about manufacturing airplanes as he did about real estate. But he loved buying planes, and he liked to tinker with the engines and tweak their wing and flap designs. In the mid-2000s, he decided to buy what he calls a "hot-rod plane"— capable of high speeds and long range—from a company called Phoenix Air. Before he could buy the plane, the company ran into financial troubles. Jack loved the plane so much he bought the company.

He set up shop in Port St. Lucie, a blue-collar town north of Palm Beach that had a convenient and cheap airport. Warner invested $250,000 in the company and borrowed another $250,000 from a friend. They spent the next year developing a new prototype and building a manufacturing line.

In between his nights at Teasers and his days flying planes and hanging out with naked strippers at his pool, Warner thought he had found the perfect retirement.

"I was done," he said. "Simple as that. I thought I was set. I thought I'd never have to worry about money again."

Sure, there was talk of a real estate bubble, especially in Florida. Jack heard plenty about the speculators and the no-money-down mortgages and the overbuilding. But Lucky's Landing seemed a sure bet. Development in and around Key West area has been frozen for decades with restrictive zoning, so no one could build a new structure without tearing down an old one (assuming they got permission). Lucky's Landing had the space to build forty-six new homes.

He could even transfer the building rights to a buyer at another location. The rights alone could be sold for $250,000 each—even if he didn't build a single house. Lucky's Landing was appraised by multiple lenders and brokers at more than $14 million.

"Did I think anything could go wrong? Of course I did. Maybe the real estate market would fall. Maybe we'd have a recession. But even if that happened, I figured I'd be fine. There was such a big cushion. The property was valued at $14 million. And I had only a small amount of debt compared to its value. That's what I thought anyway."

THE MIDDLE-CLASS MILLIONAIRES

Jack Warner was a "middle-class millionaire," someone who worked his way up from poverty by starting his own business. He was a ditchdigger, and a great one at that.

Yet like so many of the modestly wealthy (those with between $1 million and $10 million in wealth) over the past thirty years, Jack was swept up by the post-1982 wave of financial speculation and investment bubbles. He became convinced of his own market savvy in areas of the economy where he had no experience. He joined the nation's headlong rush toward ever-greater wealth, ever-bigger homes and boats, and trophy mates. And he traded in his steady-earning business, the excavation firm, for a chance at bigger, easier riches. Like the Sterns and others, he went from being a wealth builder to an asset trader. So many other people were making instant millions by flipping real estate and companies, why couldn't he?

In the world of high-beta wealth, however, it is often these lesser millionaires who get hurt the most. People like the Siegels, who went from billionaires to millionaires, will see their lives change on the margins, even if they perceive the changes as more severe. They are still lifetime residents of Richistan.

Jack Warner had less of a cushion. The middle-class millionaires barely made it to the top rungs of the wealth ladder and were hanging on by their fingertips. They had little to stop their fall to the bottom. A study of Americans with $1.5 million or more in investable assets found that more than half will continue working into retirement. Another study found that nearly half of today's millionaires are worried about outliving their assets and said they would have to change their lifestyle in retirement.

Jack's story offers lessons to the mass of Americans who hope to become wealthy without getting caught in the traps of high-beta wealth. The keys to avoiding ruin today are to stick to your business specialty, borrow for your business and not your lifestyle, and always value your assets based on long-term price trends rather than short-term bubble valuations. Most of all, never, ever sell assets at the bottom of a cycle if you can avoid it.

THE JOYS OF BORROWING

Debt was always a friend to Jack Warner. At Warner and Sons, he was always borrowing as much as he could from banks to buy new equipment or hire new workers to try to win more contracts. He also used borrowed money for homes, cars, and planes. Leverage was his fuel, and it seemed endlessly renewable. He never paid the money back on time, always keeping it until the minute the bank threatened to place him in default. The lax lending practices and low interest rates of the past thirty years made debt a necessity for anyone wanting to get rich.

"If I can borrow at 2 percent and put that money in my business and make 10 percent, it's stupid not to borrow," he says. "Maybe I was always a little close to the edge. But I always made it work."

Jack's friend Paul put it more bluntly. "Jack was always stretched too thin," he says. "He borrowed to the max. That's just the way he is."

When Jack bought Lucky's, he borrowed $800,000 of the $1.025 million price. He then borrowed another $1 million to improve the property, tear down the trailer park, and build his house. He had an additional $1 million in liens from business partners and contractors, bringing his total debts to nearly $3 million. The loans were larger than any Jack had ever taken before. But they were still minor compared to the market value of the property and his potential borrowings: Marine Bank of the Florida Keys valued the property at over $14 million and offered to bankroll $25 million of the costs for the new development.

In hindsight, $3 million in debt looks excessive. At the time, it seemed conservative. "Even if the value of the property fell by more than half, I would still be fine," Jack said. "And nothing like that had ever happened in the Keys, so it didn't seem possible."

In 2007, when the real estate market in Florida started its rapid slide, the bank called his $1.8 million loan. "Of course I didn't have the money," he said. "The bank was crazy to think I did. But they were even more crazy to call the loan. They knew the place was worth $14 million."

Jack's airplane business was also having trouble getting off the ground. He had built a prototype and had a full manufacturing line constructed inside a hangar in northern Florida. Yet on the day of the company's maiden flight, the test pilot called in sick. Jack decided to do the test flight himself. He had a smooth take-off, but when he got into the air he forgot which way he had set the thruster. Instead of easing up on the throttle, he gave it full power, which blew out the engine. Suddenly he was a thousand feet above the ocean with no power.

Jack guided the plane back to the airport and hit the runway hard, breaking the landing gear and shattering large chunks of the fuselage. He injured his back, which had already been broken in a previous plane crash.

With the bank demanding payment of his entire loan, Jack headed back to the Keys and started selling off everything he owned. He sold off his Boss Hoss trike, which he bought for $40,000, for $12,000. He sold his Cessna for $125,000. He sold the Corvette, the Harley-Davidson, and other toys for less than half what he paid. He shut down the plane business and offered it for sale, though no one wanted to buy a smashed-up prototype and a hangar full of parts—especially at a time when unsold planes were piling up around the country.

"I just went for broke," Jack says. "I kept thinking, 'This can't be happening to me.' One day I'm worth $20 million and the bank is promising me $25 million more, and the next day I'm selling my TVs and furniture to raise cash. It was just so quick."

Hope came in the form of an auction. While he hated to lose Lucky's, he figured the bank would get a good price for it at auction. Early estimates were that the property and his house would sell for $4 million to $5 million. That would still leave him with at least $1 million after paying back the loan.

Jack called old friends, business contacts, and investors to drum up interest in the sale. The auction company launched its own marketing blitz. A few days before the auction, in August 2008, Warner got the good news that more than fourteen people were planning to bid.

On the morning of the auction, he was confident he would bounce back. He went to his favorite breakfast joint, the Big Pine

Café, and had his favorite breakfast, a towering stack of pancakes with peanut butter.

By late morning he started to worry. Not a single person had registered to bid. He found out the auctioneer was insisting on selling the house and development property as one piece, even though the two properties appealed to different types of buyers.

The auction was supposed to start at 1:00 p.m., but there were no bidders. At one-thirty they had to start. Two local residents— a doctor and retiree—showed up at the last minute and registered to bid. The price started at $1 million and slowly crept up: $1.5 million, $1.8 million, $2 million. At $2.4 million the bidding came to a stop. The two bidders turned to each other and agreed to team up, with one getting the house and the other the development.

The hammer came down at $2.5 million. After commissions and other payments, the sale price left Jack with more than $1 million in debt. Jack Warner was officially broke.

"I fell into my chair and just sat there," he said. "It hit me pretty hard. What would I do? Where would I go? How would I survive?"

SLEEPING IN THE PICKUP

On a rainy afternoon in the winter of 2010, Jack is sitting at the counter of the Airport Tiki restaurant at the Port St. Lucie International Airport in Florida. A blond waitress named Jeannie comes over to take his order.

"Surprise me," he says.

Despite its name, Airport Tiki doesn't have much tiki nor much of an airport. It's a yellow-walled diner located at the Port

St. Lucie airport, a landing strip and refueling stop for recreational fliers going to or coming back from the Bahamas.

During the good times, Jack used to stop in at the Tiki for a burger as he was flying through on the way to Bermuda or the Keys. Later he came here when he was building his Phoenix airplanes, located in a hangar nearby. Now he arrives most mornings in his pickup truck for the cheap breakfast.

As he sits at the counter, in paint-stained cargo shorts, a blue T-shirt, and worn-out sneakers, his cell phone rings. "Hello?" he says. "Okay, what debt are you trying to collect?" He quickly hangs up.

Jack gets these calls all day, from banks, credit card companies, auto lenders, lawyers. He gives them all the same answer: "Stand in line, buddy. There's nothing to collect."

Ever since the sale of Lucky's, Jack has been jobless. That's partly by choice, since any salary would just go straight to the creditors. He considered filing for bankruptcy but decided it would be far too complicated and costly.

He does odd jobs for money, usually making $40 to $50 a day fixing toilets or repairing roofs. He sleeps in his pickup truck—a 2002 GMC with more than 200,000 miles—or sometimes on the couches of friends.

His eventual plan is to live off Social Security payments, which are off-limits to creditors and which he'll start receiving in 2011. "I never dreamed I'd be living off Social Security," he says. As for trying to get rich again, he says, "It's not going to happen for me."

While driving to one of his jobs, I ask Warner what he's worth. He pulls out his wallet and counts the bills. "Fifty-three dollars," he said. "You caught me on a good day. Yesterday I was worth $9."

Around Port St. Lucie, Jack doesn't talk much about his millionaire past and—this being Florida—no one asks or really cares. He's just "Handyman Jack." And that's fine with him.

———

"A few days ago, I was fixing a toilet for a guy who owned a condo on the beach," he says. "He probably paid $1 million for this condo, and he was real arrogant. He starts telling me, 'Do this, do that,' and getting nasty. I just looked at him and smiled and said, 'Would you like to fix it?' And he shut up. It didn't matter to me. Because I can just walk away."

Jack insists he's happier now that money no longer rules his life.

"Before, when I had money, I was always worried about paying people, or moving money around, or making a sale, or raising enough money from investors. I was responsible for so many people and so many things. I was always going from one meeting or phone call to another, and life was passing by. Sure, I enjoyed myself. But I look back now and realize I never really spent time with my family. I never really knew my kids. I regret that. I feel bad about that.

"It's a cliché, but wealth doesn't do much for you. What makes me happy are my friends—the friends I have left, the real friends."

Paul Shannon, Jack's former flying buddy, said he admires Jack's ability to carry on despite the losses and the complete collapse of his personal life. When the money ran out, so did the girls, the toys, and many of Jack's so-called friends. "To lose that kind of money so quickly and to be able to keep your chin up blows my mind," Paul says. "I don't know anybody else who could do it. There was a period of time when I was worried about him. He was really depressed, and I thought he might do something to himself. I still sometimes worry."

Paul has tried to convert Jack to Christianity, with no success. "Jack's just not spiritual in that way. But somehow he finds his inspiration somewhere."

Jack says it's his connections with his few remaining friends and family that keep him going, along with meaningful work.

For a few hours each day, he does volunteer construction work at a drug and alcohol rehabilitation center for men just outside Port St. Lucie. He says he's never had any addictions. But Jack likes helping out his friend who founded the center, and feels like he's helping people in need. He's also helping to build a second rehab center for addicted women.

"Jack only sees the upside," says Paul. "That's part of why he was so successful. If he's taking on debt or trusting other people or starting a business, he doesn't see the risks. He just sees the good. He trusts that it will all work out, and he jumps right in. I just hope that optimism stays with him."

As he drives his pickup truck to his next job—fixing a dog fence for $20—Jack turns up the radio and rolls down the window to let in the rain. "I've got one job right now, to fix this fence," he says. "After that, the world is wide open. I have nowhere to go, nowhere to be, no one that I have to kiss up to in a meeting. It's just me and my truck and my $53. That's all I really need."

5

THE MAKE-BELIEVE BILLIONAIRE

In 2009, Edra Blixseth took the remaining members of her household staff for a walk down her driveway. There were about thirty of them—cleaning ladies, gardeners, security guards, cooks, and a driver. Some had worked for her for more than a decade. They walked in a quiet column in the chilly desert morning until they reached the front gate.

Edra thanked them all for their years of dedicated service. She gave them each a hug and a kiss. Then, one by one, she fired them.

After the last cleaning lady had walked out, Edra closed the gate. She looked back at her 240-acre estate with its own golf course and 30,000-square-foot mansion, and she burst out laughing.

"I was just staring at this 240 acres and thinking, 'I'm it.' There was no one to help me. It was funny at first. Then it was terrifying."

Her most immediate problem was maintaining the property, one of the most elaborate and labor-dependent private estates in the country. Porcupine Creek, her desert palace near Palm Springs, had neither porcupines nor a natural creek, but it did have a golf course with more than a million flowers, plus artificial rivers, waterfalls, and imported grass. Her main house had ten bathrooms, five kitchens, a full-size movie theater, and a commercial-size spa. Then there were the seven themed guest villas (including the Tiki Villa, the Hollywood Villa, and the Rocky Mountain Villa), along with the amphitheater, the outdoor carousel, and the vast collection of computers, lighting systems, television screens, alarm systems, communication networks, and audio components that kept the hotel-like home operating.

Edra was also worried about her own security. They had always had a team of guards, led by one of former president Gerald Ford's Secret Service chiefs, surrounding the property. The estate had a concrete wall and an alarm system. But the property border was too big and porous for the wall and alarm system to protect it completely. And the alarms were connected to the phones, which had been cut off because she couldn't pay the bill.

"I'm totally exposed," Edra told me, staring out across the golf course and the orange desert as the sun began to set. "There's very little to stop someone if they really want to get in."

Beyond the fear of intruders or the logistics of trying do the work of 110 staffers, Edra faced a more profound and lasting fear: that of suddenly having to do things for herself.

For more than twenty-five years, she had a retinue of cooks, maids, drivers, pilots, yacht stewards, gardeners, security guards, estate managers, butlers, waiters, masseuses, fashion consultants, PR people, and personal assistants to handle her every need. Each morning, her award-winning German chef sent up coffee, lemon water, and the newspaper to her bedside. Her cleaning staff kept every gold faucet freshly polished and every bar of soap new and freshly wrapped in French paper bearing the home's porcupine logo. She would press a button on her cell phone or radio and have a driver at the ready. Her wine or vodka glasses were never empty. She hadn't made her own bed, gone grocery shopping, or done her own dishes in years.

Edra was capable of doing these things. Or at least she used to be before she and her husband became rich. Yet over time, the forces of wealth had lifted her so far above the world of everyday human survival skills that she had to relearn them all. She was like a billionaire's version of Rip Van Winkle, suddenly waking from a decades-long dependence on supplicants and discovering a strange new world of grocery stores, airport lines, and toilet scrubbers.

"It's not like I wasn't able to do any of these things," Edra says, groping in the entry hall for a light switch, which used to be operated by a smart-home software system controlled by her staff. "But we always employed all these people to do things for us. And if we tried to do anything ourselves, they took it as an insult. It was threatening their job to do something myself."

As Edra tells it, her return to the real world started out as a comedy of errors. After driving herself around in her ten-year-old Mercedes, she discovered she was running out of gas. She pulled into a filling station, then spent ten minutes trying to operate the self-service gas pump with its credit card reader. Eventually she gave up and paid cash.

When she needed cheap clothes for her grandkids, she found herself in the uncharted aisles of Target and Marshalls. "I never knew about this place called Marshalls," she said. "It's amazing. I can't believe I had never heard of it."

Grocery shopping, on the other hand, gave her sticker shock. "I used to ask the chef why he was spending so much on food, like $150 or $300 per delivery," she said. "Our monthly food bills were easily in the thousands. But when I went to the store myself, I was surprised at how much things cost. I mean, one organic tomato for $2?"

She tried to make the most of her household chores. Her hours spent every morning pulling weeds on the golf course became "Zen weeding," giving her a mental break from the endless lawsuits and depositions she faced during the rest of her day. She found that driving herself could be surprisingly liberating, as long as she wasn't getting gas. Her time in the kitchen allowed her to try to resurrect some old favorite recipes. Giving me a tour of her walk-in refrigerator, Edra pointed to a baking dish filled with a wrinkly, slightly green-hued eggplant parmigiana. "I made that myself," she said, beaming. "It was delicious. Really. I guess it looked better the day I made it."

One morning Edra and I were sitting on the patio outside her mansion. She was holding a roll of paper towels and a bottle of Windex, which had become her favorite accessory now that the staff was gone. Like Jack Warner, she talked about how losing money had been something of a blessing, allowing her to reconnect with the real world, revealing her true friends, and giving her a new perspective on the everyday struggles of other Americans.

She said that if she ever wrote a book about her experiences, it would be called *Fall to Grace*, since her dramatic reversal of fortune had been a spiritual redemption of sorts rather than a purgatory. Material things no longer mattered as much, she said. What mattered was living a more real, healthy life, with true friends and family.

"I'm living my life now more as the person I am, not a person I am pretending to be," she says. "My big goal going forward is to be genuine. I want a genuine life."

In the middle of her elegy to the simple life, I asked her if losing wealth had actually made her happier than living with wealth.

Edra laughed. "Are you kidding? No way. Anyone who says they're happier without money is lying. I still want the comforts I used to have. And I hope to get some of them back. They make life a lot easier. And they give you freedom and choices. But what I've learned is that you can't let things and stuff define you. That's where I went wrong." And with that, Edra looked at her watch and noticed that it was lunchtime. "Right now," she says "I would be a lot happier if I had my chef back."

The rise and fall of Tim and Edra Blixseth has many parallels to the high-beta stories of the Siegels and Jack Warner. Like the Siegels, they got caught up in the status race and spending binge of the 2000s with little regard for the long-term costs or consequences. Like Jack Warner, they were blue-collar climbers who pulled themselves up from poverty with a steady but unglamorous business, then got seduced by the asset bubbles and wealth glorification of the 2000s.

For Jack Warner, the Siegels, and the Blixseths, debt was the ultimate wealth destroyer.

Yet the Blixseth story is an extreme among extremes, showing just how suddenly and violently wealth can be made and lost in the age of high-beta wealth. Jack Warner, for all his misfortune, never climbed all that high on the wealth ladder relative to today's wealth standards. He went from a few million dollars in net worth to a theoretical net worth of $14 million, then back down to zero. Even though he hit rock bottom, he fell from the place I called Lower Richistan (inhabited by those with a mere $10 million or so) rather than the more lofty heights of Upper Richistan.

As for the Siegels, they climbed much higher than Warner. But they won't fall nearly as low. Yes, they will probably lose the largest home in America along with their fleet of jets and army of nannies. But they will still wind up multimillionaires because of the value of their private company and assets. The Siegels' beta was higher than Warner's, but still within the statistical band of many of today's boom-and-bust wealthy. Edra's beta, on the other hand, would be off the charts in any diagram. In a matter of two years, she went from being a billionaire to bust, from living large to liquidation, and from having one of the most expensive homes in the country to having no home at all. If anyone can claim to have gone from rags to riches and back to rags (at least on paper), it's Edra Blixseth.

In the past, stories such as Edra's were the freak results of fraud or theft. They were the Madoff investors who lost their life savings, who one day they thought they were millionaires or even billionaires and the next day learned they had nothing. They were the finance-challenged celebrities, pop stars, or athletes. Such radical downward mobility is not considered "real" in the sense that it rarely reflects broader economic trends or changes.

Yet Edra's fall is the product of larger economic change. In her case, the primary forces behind high-beta wealth—debt, spending, asset bubbles—all converged to create one of the defining examples of modern wealth destruction and volatility. She and Tim rode on the very top of the asset bubble, with maximum leverage and a defiant lifestyle. As we will see, when the debt came due and the asset bubble popped, the Blixseths didn't have enough savings or real assets to pay their creditors. The problems were made worse by a more traditional wealth destroyer: divorce.

What is most striking about the Blixseths, however, is the impact that high-beta wealth had on their lives. Their identities, values, and happiness were shaped as much by their precarious rise as by their sudden collapse. In the end, Tim and Edra came out of the experience with vastly different outcomes.

If you ask Tim and Edra Blixseth what lessons they learned

after losing so much money so quickly, you will get two very different answers.

Tim's answer is simple: "Don't get a divorce in the middle of a recession."

He will tell you that his entire financial mess and the blizzard of lawsuits and bad press of the past four years was largely the result of his nasty battle with his wife. He will tell you how she mismanaged money and engaged in a conspiracy to take over the Yellowstone Club. He will explain, in the entertaining and briefly convincing way that only Tim can manage, that the main villains in their epic downfall were the bankers who lent him too much money—$375 million, to be exact.

He will explain that he still has his jet, his 150,000 acres of timberland, his Mexican resort, the private island in the Turks and Caicos, and his yacht. He will muse about his next big fortune from a reality TV show or a natural gas reserve. He's married again, to a slim, young blonde from Seattle, and he remains close to his two children from his first marriage.

For Tim, the past four years appear as just another momentary setback in a life defined by redemption and rebounds. "I'm happier than I've ever been," he says, looking tanned and fit on a wintry day in New York.

Edra's answer to the question about lessons is less sanguine. "Lessons? I could write a book about the lessons from all this. I'd have to go back a few years, maybe more than a few years, to start to answer."

She would probably start in Oregon in the 1970s, when Tim and Edra first met. He was an upstart land buyer who had grown up poor in rural Oregon. He couldn't afford college and he needed to support his family, so he went into the business of buying and selling timberland. He'd scoop up scattered parcels for low prices, then assemble them into larger plots he could sell to the big timber companies for a profit.

Edra grew up in a more middle-class family in California's San Joaquin Valley. She was always ambitious; she says one of her happiest moments was winning a competition to bring other kids to Sunday school. "I won a Snickers bar," she said. "I didn't do it for just the Snickers bar. I did it for the challenge. I have always found fulfillment in meeting a challenge."

But her life took a sudden turn when she got pregnant in high school and married at the age of seventeen. "It was kind of clichéd—one day after cheerleading practice, with number 10 on the football team," she says.

She worked the graveyard shift at a diner to pay the bills. Later, she managed a restaurant and helped launch a chain of restaurant-inns. She met Tim at one of her restaurants when they were both trying to get out of bad marriages.

They were both ambitious, entrepreneurial, and attracted to the finer things in life. Edra drove a Mercedes. Tim's dream was to one day have enough money to pay cash for a new Rolls-Royce. Edra wanted a home big enough for their four kids and, one day, their grandkids.

They married and settled down, and in 1982 they bought a 10,000-square-foot historic home in Portland. They got their first plane. Yet behind the façade of wealth, the Blixseths were always living close to the edge. They were putting most of their money back into their business, even as their lifestyle became more and more expensive.

"It always looked like we had more than we really had," Edra says. "There was always pressure to maintain our lifestyle. We were always living beyond our means."

One Christmas Eve they had no money for presents for their kids, even though they lived in a mansion. They rushed to cash a check from a logging company, drove three hours to a Toys R Us to buy presents, and raced home to put them under the tree.

In the 1980s, Tim's business crashed after a fall in timber prices. He and Edra declared both personal and corporate bankruptcy, leaving creditors with $17 million in bad debt.

They were quickly back on their feet, forming a new timber company shortly after the bankruptcy. The Blixseths later sold it for more than $20 million. They moved to Lake Tahoe and bought their first yacht, a 97-foot Feadship, along with a Citation jet.

After selling the company, Tim went into semi-retirement. He started a music company, building on his minor success as a songwriter in the 1970s with a tune called "I Hope to Find Your Rainbow." But his real windfall came a few years later, courtesy of the federal government.

In 1991, the Blixseths swapped the government some of their timberland for a 13,500-acre parcel near Yellowstone National Park. The Yellowstone land turned out to be one of the most stunning and valuable pieces of property in the country. The Blixseths turned the property into the Yellowstone Club, an exclusive compound deep in the Montana Rockies where the rich could ski, golf, drink, and play without having to mingle with the non-rich. Members paid $250,000 to join and millions more to buy property and build homes on the site.

It was the ultimate in pampered mountaineering, and part of the sudden gentrification of the Rockies that turned towns such as Jackson Hole, Wyoming, and Sun Valley, Idaho, into high-elevation versions of the Hamptons. At the Yellowstone Club, members could have ski boots pre-warmed before their arrival, their log mansions were always filled with groceries and wine, and their dogs were given hand-sliced meat by the Yellowstone staff.

With Tim's sales charm and Edra's expert operating skills, the club membership exploded with newly rich Wall Streeters, entrepreneurs, sports stars, real estate developers, cable magnates, and dot-com billionaires. Bill Gates became a member, along with hotelier Barry Sternlicht and former vice president Dan Quayle. The membership swelled to more than three hundred.

Land started selling for more than $1 million an acre. Some members started buying parcels and flipping them for instant fortunes. By 2005, the Yellowstone Club was appraised at more than $1.2 billion. Tim and Edra, who owned virtually all of the club, were now billionaires, at least on paper. To make it official, in 2005 Tim debuted on the *Forbes* 400 list of richest Americans, his wealth estimated at $1.2 billion.

The Blixseths had always lived large. But by 2006, fueled by their $1 billion in paper wealth and ever-rising real estate values, their lifestyle became epic. They bought three jets—one for him, one for her, and one for friends and family. Porcupine Creek became their home base and grand trophy. The Blixseths also had homes in Seattle, Cabo San Lucas, and Montana. They threw $1.5 million weddings for their kids, with the flowers for one daughter's wedding costing $250,000.

Tim not only achieved his dream of buying a brand new Rolls-Royce for cash but bought two—one Phantom painted in flashy two-tone colors so that he would get good valet parking spots at restaurants, and another in simple blue for "just driving around," he said.

To the public, the Blixseths were living the ultimate American dream. Privately, however, their lives were starting to spin out of control.

Edra had always loved parties and drinking and getting together with friends. But in 2005 and 2006, Tim says, her drinking got worse. She admits that she had a drinking problem and says she drank to drown her problems with Tim, who was rarely around and had become more distant. He was also becoming increasingly crazed with money and the need for attention, buying ever larger cars, boats, planes, and properties, she said.

While they both liked the good life, their priorities and rationale for their riches began to diverge. Porcupine Creek became the center of many battles. Edra saw the home as the center of their family, a place where her kids, grandkids, and growing ranks of close friends could all live and enjoy life together. She felt deep pride in its design, since she had picked out almost every lamp, tile, and ceiling fresco. She took special pride in their antique wooden bed, which came from the archbishop of Milan's quarters and had a carved Jesus above Tim's side and a carved Mary above Edra's.

"I don't think of it as this big house with guest villas and a golf course," Edra says. "I think of it as home."

Tim saw it differently. To him, Porcupine Creek was a marketing vehicle used to wine and dine the rich and powerful and get them to buy properties at the fledgling Yellowstone Club.

"The idea was if they could see what Edra and I could create at Porcupine Creek, they'd sign up for Yellowstone," Tim said. "It was a business tool, a great business tool. I always saw Porcupine Creek as an investment."

Tim also hated having so many staffers hanging around.

"I never liked a bunch of people in my house," he said. "It was like a hotel. I resented that even back then."

Edra and Tim also fought about spending. Even as he preached the simple life, saying to all who would listen that "if you're defined by your things, you're not defined," he continued to pile up toys. So did Edra, but she felt more conflicted. She turned to Buddhism and Eastern religions, looking to fill a growing void in her life.

Edra recalls a turning point in 2006, when she and Tim were

sitting on the patio of Porcupine Creek after dinner. She asked him if he wanted to take a sunset stroll with her through the gardens. Tim refused. It was a seemingly small request, but for Edra it meant the end of their marriage.

"He just didn't want to be with me or to do anything that I wanted to do," she says. Edra ran to the bathroom and started crying. It was at that moment that she realized two things: that she wanted a divorce, and that she was too afraid of getting a divorce because she might lose the house.

"I said to myself in the bathroom, 'If I could keep Porcupine Creek, I wouldn't stay married.' I was willing to stay married and miserable in order to keep Porcupine Creek. After that, I couldn't look at myself in the mirror. I wanted to keep the status quo. I sacrificed who I was for something that was material. So yes, you could say I got caught up in all the stuff."

The Blixseths' financial situation had undergone a radical shift in 2005, when they took out a mammoth loan. Credit Suisse, the Swiss-based investment bank, approached them about taking cash out of Yellowstone in the form of a business loan. Over several wine-filled dinners, the Credit Suisse team said they had just structured a loan for the owner of another resort and could promise the Blixseths $150 million. The Yellowstone Club would be the collateral for the loan.

Initially Tim and Edra were cool to the idea. The club was generating plenty of cash and the Blixseths didn't really need the money, even with their outsize personal spending. They also knew the perils of debt from their last bankruptcy. Tim and Edra had promised each other they would never get into debt trouble again.

"Debt is the root of all evil," Tim always said, and still says today.

Yet the loan came with an irresistible hook: it was non-recourse. That meant Tim and Edra would never be held personally liable for the loan, even if they never paid back a cent. If the club crashed, which seemed unlikely, Tim and Edra would walk away with their planes, cars, homes, and yachts untouched.

"It's not really my debt if it's non-recourse," Tim said. "That was the cornerstone of the deal. It was the depersonalization of debt."

The land sales from Yellowstone Club would easily cover the interest and principal. And Tim told Edra that even if they wound up short of cash, they wouldn't be responsible.

"Tim's answer was always, 'We don't have to pay it back,'" Edra says. "We were taking some money off the table."

It seemed like the deal of the century—until Credit Suisse came back and offered them even more money. The bank said investor demand for such loans was so strong that they were offering to give the Blixseths $230 million. Like many commercial loans, the Blixseth deal was "syndicated," or sliced up and sold off to other investors.

Days before the loan deal was supposed to be signed, Credit Suisse came back to Tim. They had a problem. The bank had so many investors wanting to buy pieces of the Blixseth loan that they needed to increase the size. They asked Tim if he would take $375 million.

"We said no, but they kept pressing," Tim says. "So I said 'Okay, but that's it, no more.'"

It was a typical loan of the Wall Street–fueled real estate bubble—huge fees for the underwriter, a pile of cash for the lender, and a ticking time bomb for the investors and property owners (in this case club members). Credit Suisse made more than $7 million in fees from the deal. A judge later ruled that Credit Suisse's due diligence on the deal was all but nonexistent and that its $1.2 billion valuation for the Yellowstone Club was based on a highly questionable appraisal.

Edra says she was always opposed to borrowing so much money. "If we had gotten $150 million, we could have handled it. Even $220 million. But $375 million? No way. I knew it was way too much money."

Yet the Blixseths (Edra included) had no trouble finding ways to spend their sudden windfall. The loan documents expressly allowed the Blixseths to use up to $209 million for their own personal benefit. To avoid paying taxes on the money, the Blixseths recorded the $209 million as a personal loan from the Yellowstone Club. They signed an IOU to the club promising to pay it back. While the move saved them millions in taxes, it would later come back to haunt them.

They paid off their mortgage on Porcupine Creek, paid off their Gulfstream jets, and put a few million into personal bank accounts and other businesses.

They launched a new venture called Yellowstone Club World, a global version of the Yellowstone Club where rich members could vacation at one of ten palatial private resorts around the world. The Blixseths went on one of the most extravagant real estate shopping sprees in history, picking up a medieval castle in France, a private island and mansion in the Turks and Caicos, a golf resort in Mexico, and a chunk of land in Scotland to build a golf course. To get to all the new locations, they bought a second yacht.

Edra accepts some blame for the loan. "How could I not feel some responsibility for it? I benefited from the lifestyle, no question. And I would say that I was part of the problem because I went against my better instincts. One of my kids told me at the time, 'Mom, you went to the dark side.' I stopped fighting this need for more and more money and material things."

She would often remind Tim during the loan deal that "this

is exactly the kind of thing we said we'd never do" after their last bankruptcy.

Even if the loan did go bad and they had to pay it back, the Blixseths had so many valuable assets, they assumed they could never get caught short. Yellowstone was appraised at $1.2 billion and Porcupine Creek had been valued at more than $200 million, plus they had thousands of acres of land and developments that were easily worth hundreds of millions. How could $375 million wipe out more than $1.5 billion in assets? It just didn't seem possible, even if the economy went into recession.

Yet as Tim kept spending and expanding, Edra grew more anxious. She felt like their lives had become a lie, since few people knew about the loan. If the real estate market tanked, she thought, they would be unable to make the loan payments and Credit Suisse could take the club.

"I felt like we had to keep up this façade of not having any debt or financial pressures," she said.

Tim says he became fed up with her drinking. One morning, after a night of partying, Tim announced he was leaving. Edra said, "You owe me one more hour of your time." She sat him down in her office and made him watch a one-hour video by Tony Robbins, the motivational speaker. In the video, Robbins talked about the importance of being true to ourselves. For Tim, "It was the longest hour of my life."

After it was over, Tim hugged her and drove off with nothing but his toothbrush. He later wrote a song about their marriage, with these lyrics:

> We had everything the world could see but love.
> Sip by sip she slipped away
> From my heart and then my days.

Initially, Tim and Edra tried to keep the divorce civil and private. But like many divorces involving rich people, it quickly devolved into a spectacle of public attacks and money battles. Tim accused Edra of being a steroid-addicted alcoholic who had a long history of overspending. He said she had flown her house cleaner on the Gulfstream to their various properties and spent $90,000 on a divorce party that featured Tim's likeness on voodoo dolls and rolls of toilet paper.

"She has been recklessly spending money as if it grows on trees," he said in one press release, urging a Montana court to liquidate her assets.

In the spring of 2008, the Blixseths put the Yellowstone Club up for sale and inked a deal for $400 million. It fell through as the real estate market crashed. Property sales at the Yellowstone Club ground to a halt.

With their business collapsing, the Blixseths settled their divorce by dividing up all their holdings. Edra got the club, Porcupine Creek, and the French castle. Tim got the Mexican resort, the Turks and Caicos property, and tens of millions of dollars in cash.

Along with the club and the house, Tim also gave Edra the most important item on their balance sheet: the Credit Suisse debt. She agreed to take over the promissory note that she and Tim had signed saying they owed the club $209 million.

Edra said it seemed like a fair deal at the time. She planned to sell their French castle to keep Yellowstone running until she could turn around the business or find a buyer. Yet the deal to sell the castle to a Russian oligarch collapsed and she ran out of cash. Yellowstone filed for bankruptcy in 2008 and sold for about $100 million—less than 10 percent of its appraised value in 2005. Because she was personally on the hook for $209 million, she filed for Chapter 7 personal bankruptcy.

Tim appears to have escaped any real damage from their financial wreck. Even though he's being chased by creditors demanding his properties to pay back the loan, Tim shows little regrets for his spending spree, his lifestyle, his debt, or the long line of angry club members and former business partners who are suing him or no longer talking to him. If he went a little too far during the good times, well, so had plenty of other rich people.

"It was fun back in the go-go years, to have all the stuff you don't need and always wanted," he said. "Anyone who says they didn't have fun isn't telling the truth. The whole world was living like that."

Edra had more of a reckoning, both financially and psychologically. Back when she was rich, her daughter would joke about Edra's fantasyland of privilege and isolation. It was a world unto itself, she said, one that Edra fully controlled and yet one that also failed to give Edra some of the real connections—to people, to family, to experiences—that she so craved. During one conversation, Edra made a joke about a politician who needed to "get back to the real world."

"Real world?" her daughter asked. "Mom, you don't live in the real world. You live on a 240-acre estate surrounded by guards and a staff of a hundred people. You only see the people you want to see and friends you want to invite over. You leave the FBO [fixed base operator, or private jet terminal] in Palm Springs, then you go to the FBO in Yellowstone Club, which you own. Then you see more of the same people that you only want to see. That's your life. Mom, you know I love you. But you don't live in the real world."

Edra's grasp of the real world has improved. But along with the newfound respect for gas stations and grocery lines, she's also living with loss—especially of friends and family. When she was wealthy, Edra felt she had a tight circle of real friends who didn't care about the money or playing on her private golf course but liked her for who she was. There was another group of friends who liked her for her charitable donations, parties, and free trips on her private plane. Yet Edra figured they were a small minority—maybe 10 percent of her friends—and that she knew exactly who they were. "I could spot them immediately," she said. "You develop a very good radar for these kinds of people."

Her radar, however, proved woefully inaccurate when it came to wealth loss. She expected to lose only about 10 percent of her friends after her bankruptcy. Instead, she's lost more than half. "I still don't really know why," she says. "These are people who were never about the money. Or at least I don't think they were"

She's also had a rude awakening when it comes to her family. Of the Blixseths' four children, two are Tim's from a previous marriage and two are hers from a previous marriage. She considered them all her children. Yet after the divorce, Tim's children have largely taken his side and stopped talking to Edra. Edra's daughter Julie, whom she was closest to, moved to Sweden with her family. At the very time when she needs them most, her family is largely absent.

Edra says her life has become so filled with personal attacks, lawsuits, and public scrutiny that her daughter and grandchildren felt it would be healthier to stay clear. She also says that in Sweden, "it's easier to live with less."

"The family separating was the biggest shock," she says. "I got used to having them around. And I think that it would in some ways be easier to face these pressures if I had them here. But it's just not possible."

You might think that after her fall, Edra would have the lessons of the past four years ingrained in her memory. And yet, when I ask her about her biggest fear for the future, she has a surprising response.

"My biggest fear is that I forget what happened and that I forget the lessons," she said. "Maybe that sounds weird in light of the extreme change in my life. But I think that this crisis might have been too quick and too easy for some of the wealthy. Nothing really changed. Now, I don't think you'll be seeing the Credit Suisse–type loans for a while. And I don't think real estate prices will go up like they did. But we have short memories in this country. For the wealthy, nothing really changed. That means it could all happen again. My fear is that I forget all of this. My fear is that we all forget."

A PERVERSION OF VALUE

Some of the wealthy will be permanently changed by the decade's wealth shocks. There are people like Warner, who because of age and debts, will never climb back. Yet there are also people like John McAfee, who now looks at the whole notion of wealth, spending, and quality of life in a different way.

McAfee founded McAfee Associates, a computer security company best known for its anti-virus software. He sold his stake in the company for somewhere between $50 million to $100 million and started and sold another company for $17 million.

By the mid-2000s, he was worth more than $100 million. With his goatee, tattoos, and waves of blond hair, McAfee bears a resemblance to Richard Branson and shares his rebellious streak, openly mocking the corporate establishment while at the same time profiting from it.

After selling his businesses, McAfee devoted more time to his hobbies: racing motorcycles, flying lightweight planes over the New Mexico desert, and doing yoga. He bought homes in New Mexico, Hawaii, and Colorado.

"Success for me is, Can you wake up in the morning and feel like a twelve-year-old?" he told *Fast Company* in 2007.

By 2008, however, the money ran out on his second adolescence. His rampant spending and his costly investment decisions (including bonds sold by Lehman Brothers) drained his $100 million fortune down to just a few million. John McAfee had lost more than 95 percent of his paper net worth.

In 2008, the *New York Times* ran an article about McAfee and his efforts to auction off his properties. One of the most surprising parts about the article, however, was the response. After readers posted dozens of online comments attacking McAfee as an indulgent, self-promoting, whiny rich guy who deserved no sympathy, McAfee responded with an admission: "I am not surprised by the angry attitude toward myself expressed in many of the comments," he wrote. "In fact, I have to agree with most of them."

He added, "I fully agree that I had little need for most of my toys. I spent money on houses that I seldom visited. I conspicuously consumed. A majority of America's wealthy live and act the same, not that that excuses any of my excess."

McAfee had given away almost all of his major possessions, many to charity or local communities. "Stuff, in and of itself, has little value," he wrote. "It's what we do with it that matters."

McAfee's losses changed the way he thinks about wealth. When he started out, he believed that if he just made enough money to be secure and buy the things he wanted, he'd be happier. He was happier, for a while. But the thrill soon passed. Over time, buying another house or plane just didn't excite him anymore. What excited him was starting companies. McAfee is one of those natural entrepreneurs who live to reimagine markets, invent new products, and obsessively pursue ideas that sound insane to everyone else but make perfect sense to him.

Wealth was a by-product of that process. Yet McAfee mistook

it for the goal. For him, adding wealth and things only distracted him from his deeper drive to change the world through business. It's a lesson repeated by many of the high-beta rich, and one that was costly for McAfee to learn.

"We have over time equated entrepreneurialism with the drive to accumulate wealth," McAfee said. "It's a perversion of values."

By 2011, McAfee had gone back to what he did best. He had moved to Belize and was pursuing new vaccines from jungle plants, and he had started a host of other businesses, including the nation's largest ferry company. Getting away from American consumerism and status competitions was healthy, he said. It allowed him to focus more on what mattered.

Sitting in his bedroom, looking out over a lush jungle and waterfall, McAfee told me, "I have all I need right here. I don't need anything else. I don't need much, really."

As for the rest of America, however, he said the culture of wealth was still one of "more, more, more." Like Edra, McAfee said the lessons of the crisis are likely to be quickly forgotten. High-beta wealth will become even larger and less stable.

"Nothing's changed," he said. "There's no reason to think all this won't happen again."

In our collective amnesia, the cycles of high-beta wealth will no doubt repeat themselves in the coming years. And it won't just be the wealthy who are affected. Increasingly, the highs and lows of high-beta wealth are extracting a price from the rest of the country. As we will see in the coming chapters, high-beta wealth is distorting our communities, our consumer economy, and even our government.

PART III

Trickle-Down Risks

6

BIG MONEY RUINS EVERYTHING

On an August afternoon, the soaring notes of a jazz band float across the green lawns and white-columned porches of Aspen's West End. The peaks of the Rocky Mountains rise above the trees, reaching toward the late summer rain clouds that gather almost every day around dusk. A cool breeze rolls down from the mountains, carrying the first hints of autumn and the smell of wood smoke from nearby chimneys.

On Cooper Street, a steady stream of Land Rovers and Mercedes-Benzes make their way toward a stately Victorian mansion. The cars stop and dispatch a stream of guests wearing jewels, feather boas, and towering hats. They stroll to a large tent stretched across the mansion lawn. A band plays a ragtime tune. Waiters dressed in white shirts and bow ties hold out silver trays filled with Veuve Clicquot champagne, shrimp, and fried catfish bites. Bouquets of blue lilacs, roses, and wildflowers sprout from the tables. Over the next hour, more than 270 revelers arrive to kick off Aspen's biennial Great Gatsby Party.

The guests are decked out in 1920s attire. The men wear white linen suits and vintage ties, with candy-striped shirts, knickers, and Panama hats or golf caps. They all play roles from the rich of the past—pre-Depression tycoons, suspenders-wearing "club men," and zoot-suited gangsters with dangling pocket watches.

The women wear sequined flapper dresses and low-cut silk gowns. Jewels the size of ice cubes pour down from their tanned necks and ears. The early evening breeze has brought out a few mink shawls and ermine wraps from their summer hibernation. Bobbing along the top of the crowd are jeweled cloches and headpieces piled high with white silk and feathers.

A pair of vintage cars—one yellow, one red—frame the entrance. Fred Ayarza, one of the hosts and a longtime Aspen party fixture, stands at the gate wearing a white suit and straw hat. "Hello, sweetheart, you look beautiful. . . . There you are. Love ya! . . . Now here's the nicest and most generous guy in Aspen! Hey, Bob! . . . Hi, darling. Terrific party last week."

With a broad smile and bright blue eyes, Ayarza beams with pride at the turnout. "This could be our best year yet," he says.

Shana Tyler, a curvy blond diamond dealer wearing a velvet-trimmed bustier and feather boa, clinks champagne classes with Dessire Curiel, an exotic twenty-two-year-old in a tasseled flapper dress who sells jewelry to celebrities such as Mariah Carey. "It's a bit of an older crowd," Shana says. "But boy, these guys know how to party."

Jack Crawford, a retired oil man from Texas, wears a dark suit and a lapel button that says "I did time with Al Capone." He sits at a table with a glass of champagne and chats with his brother and a few other friends about the good old days in Aspen. "I remember one of our first winters here in the 1960s. We stayed for a month and had all kinds of parties. The ratio of men to women in Aspen back then was very high, like four guys for every gal. So having a party was one way to even it out. We would invite two women for every guy."

Many of the guests are recovering from the previous night—an Italian wine-tasting bash held at one of the co-host's houses. "You have to come over," the host says. "We have an amazing kitchen—it was featured in a magazine. And we have a great home theater. I'm not bragging, we just do. Other than that, our house is pretty normal."

The chatter at the tables is filled with the typical preoccupations of the well-heeled—their travel plans for the fall, frustrations with finding good help, discussions of diets and doctors, stories of sending the kids off to college ("with two Amex Gold Cards!"), and the escalating battle between cyclists and joggers on Aspen's mountain trails.

The Gatsby hosts—there are sixteen of them—form the core of a tight-knit group of wealthy Aspenites who host what seems like a nonstop party throughout the year. There is the Shit-Kickers Ball, held in May. There is the Fishbone Grill, held in August, followed by the Beach Blanket Bingo party, the Night in Tunisia bash, and many more. Betty Weiss figures the group has at least two parties a month, "probably a lot more."

Yet of all the parties, Gatsby is the most sumptuous. In part, that's because of the outfits. One woman who attended a few years back placed a special order with the Universal Studios costume department to get the perfect ensemble. "It's the women and the costumes that really make this," says Fred Ayarza. "The men are just props."

The Gatsby party also stands out for its cost. This year's event cost more than $50,000, all paid for by the hosts. It's not held for charity. There are no causes to support, diseases to fight, or philanthropists to honor. Its sole purpose appears to be to drink, dance, and wear over-the-top costumes.

The party invitation, which featured a fake gemstone and pink feather adorning a woman's shoe, quoted a passage from F. Scott Fitzgerald's famous novel: "There was music from my neighbor's house through the summer nights. In his blue garden men and girls came and went like moths among the whispering and the champagne and stars."

That Aspen's version of the Gatsby party was held during the daytime in a remote valley of the Rocky Mountains, rather than in the evening on the sandy shores of Long Island, didn't seem to matter. Nor did the fact that there was a recession going on, with most of America looking more like Fitzgerald's derelict "valley of ashes" than the blue-gardened East Egg. The guests had all gathered to celebrate what they called "the Gatsby values"—that sumptuous combination of wealth, exclusivity, and scenic hedonism that once made the rich feel so special. They saw Gatsby as a hero. The irony of the book appeared to be largely lost on the crowd.

In Fitzgerald's book, of course, Gatsby's world was one of corruption and moral decay, a symbol of all that was wrong with the entitled, reckless wealth of the pre-crash 1920s. As Fitzgerald wrote: "They were careless people . . . they smashed up things and creatures and then retreated back into their money or their vast carelessness, or whatever it was that kept them together, and let other people clean up the mess they had made."

Yet to the guests sipping champagne on a summer lawn that afternoon in Aspen, paying homage to Gatsby seemed to be the perfect way to end the season, and an acceptable—even commendable—reaction to the troubles faced by the rest of America.

———

"Sure, times are tough. That's exactly why we should be cel-ebrating and having fun," said one guest. "That's what Gatsby was about. Enjoying life and success and sharing it with others."

Their Gatsby party was Aspen's final summer blowout, the fi-nale to an eight-week stretch of parties and festivals that has be-come even larger than Aspen's famed ski season.

Nancy Snell, the Gatsby party planner, stands near the dance floor recalling the other recent parties she's thrown in town. There was the party at one of the town's biggest mansions featuring acro-bats swinging from chandeliers. There was the Egyptian-themed party, where the hostess was dressed like Cleopatra and carried in by muscular men dressed as Nubian slaves. There was a can-can party, the beach-themed bash, and a Western-themed party fea-turing naked cowboys painted in gold leaf.

"I'm gearing up for gay ski weekend now," Nancy says. "They always have some great parties."

As the sun begins to set behind the mountains, the wind grows colder. The Gatsby guests begin to gather their gold and silver clutches and drift out of the tent. Many are heading over to the Little Nell Hotel for an early Saturday supper.

The guests stop by to congratulate Nancy on the party. "Splen-did, just splendid," says one guest. As Nancy pays the band and hurries up the cleanup crew, she looks out over the empty tent. "I was trying to capture that line in the book about 'blue gar-dens and champagne.' It's hard to do that during the day, here in Aspen. But I think we captured the spirit. I think Gatsby would have been proud."

Indeed he would have. Because behind the glitz and glamour of the Gatsby party, the wealthy of Aspen have changed the town in dramatic ways. While they have brought visible improvements and huge amounts of money, they have also created economic and social messes that have proven difficult for others to clean up.

And a town that once prided itself on its display of millionaires and billionaires is now learning the downside of depending on the high-beta rich.

THE SILVER NUGGET

The Ute Indians used to have a name for Aspen and its environs. They called it "the shining mountains." And true to its name, Aspen has long been a town defined by great wealth and shine.

In the 1800s, Jerome B. Wheeler, a wealthy Macy's department store partner and silver miner, snowshoed into town and changed its name to Aspen. He helped make silver mining Aspen's growth engine. The town's population soared to more than twelve thousand. In 1894, miners carved out a 2,054-pound nugget of silver—the largest in the world—from nearby Smuggler Mountain and paraded it through the streets of town.

Aspen's first boom was short-lived. When silver crashed in the late 1890s, so did Aspen. Its population fell to under seven hundred, and the area looked set to become another of the many Rocky Mountain ghost towns left behind in the mining bust.

Yet forty years later, another rich visionary came to town: Walter Paepcke. Walter was a Chicago tin-can magnate who had an eye for art, literature, and philosophy. His wife, Elizabeth, was a highly cultured beauty who went by the nickname "Pussy."

The Paepckes vacationed on a large ranch named Perry Park, just outside Colorado Springs. In the winter of 1939, Elizabeth Paepcke and two houseguests decided to venture to Aspen, which was rumored to have great skiing. They took a train, then drove the rest of the way through a blizzard. They stayed at the dilapidated Hotel Jerome and the next morning hitched a ride with some miners to the bottom of Ajax Mountain. After a long trek on their sealskin-covered skis, they reached the summit.

"At the top, we halted in frozen admiration," she wrote in a memoir. "In all that landscape of rock, snow and ice, there was neither print of animal nor track of man. We were alone as though the world had just been created and we its first inhabitants."

Elizabeth was hooked. Walter—who didn't join that first trip—needed more convincing. It wasn't until after World War II that Elizabeth dragged him to Aspen. He quickly saw the commercial potential. He built the town's first ski facilities—founding Aspen Ski Co. and other ventures—while Elizabeth focused on the town's cultural growth. She helped attract world-class musicians, artists, and architects. Their largest cultural creation was the Aspen Institute, which brought together the world's leading thinkers for conferences and idea festivals.

They hosted the Goethe Bicentennial Convocation, which brought two thousand people to Aspen in the summer of 1949. Dr. Albert Schweitzer spoke at the event on his only trip to the United States.

The Aspen the Paepckes envisioned was more than a ski town and winter playground for the rich. It was a cultural oasis, an "Athens of the West," where great minds could gather to contemplate the world in a peaceful setting. The Paepckes called it the "Aspen idea," which, as Walter put it, meant "a place for man's complete life . . . where he can profit by healthy, physical recreation, with facilities at hand for his enjoyment of art, music, and education."

The Aspen idea set the town apart from the other Rocky Mountain ski towns such as Vail and Breckenridge. It sprouted art galleries, poetry readings, musical performances, theaters, and a string of summer festivals that attracted some of the world's top artists and performers. It became a haven for artists, writers, ski bums, and assorted cowboy bohemians who could rail against the establishment but live a comfortable and carefree life in the mountains.

Aspen always had plenty of rich people. But they were of a certain type—quiet, older money and frizzy-haired heiresses who lived in small homes with their multiple pets. They blended easily into the Aspen scenery. Few people knew or cared who was wealthy in town.

Michael Cleverly, an artist and writer who came to town in 1972, said the old Aspen was almost entirely devoid of class distinctions. "It was the most democratic place I'd ever been to," said Cleverly, who grew up in Vermont. "There were really no class distinctions, at least none that I could see. I couldn't believe such a place could even exist. You had ski bums and rich guys and celebrities, and in Aspen, you couldn't tell the difference. No one put on airs."

Aspen also had a colorful cast of local characters. There was Ralph Jackson, a local ski bum who took to the slopes in a top hat and bearskin coat. There was Freddie "Schnickelfritz" Fisher, a bawdy clarinet player who ran a novelty shop and used to ride in the July 4 parade with a toilet float. And of course, there was Hunter Thompson, the drug-addled, gun-crazed gonzo journalist, who came to Aspen in 1960 and moved to a private compound in nearby Woody Creek.

Jack Crawford, the oil tycoon, said that during the mid-1960s he and his brother would spend an entire ski season in town without anyone asking what they did for a living. Money helped defined Aspen, but it was rarely talked about directly.

The party scene and nightlife were also devoid of velvet ropes and VIP lists. "At our parties, and at all of the parties, it was a hell of a mix," Crawford said. "You'd have a society woman next to a ski lift operator next to a construction guy. There was no strati-fication."

Michael Cleverly said the arts and culture scene in town was also accessible to everyone. A couple of his friends launched the Aspen Center for Visual Arts, which showed work by artists from around the country. The shows were free, and they would usually get a local bartender to help out, doling out wine and carrot sticks for openings. Michael also helped host the annual Art Cart soap box derby, which usually ended with a big open party.

Starting in the 1980s, however, Aspen's wealthy began to change. The quiet old money gave way to proud new money. En-trepreneurs, cable TV magnates, media tycoons, and the first wave of Wall Streeters started pouring in. A new breed of publicity-seeking celebrities, such as Don Johnson and Ivana Trump, came to town.

Speaking at a conference in 1987, an aged Elizabeth Paepcke warned of the ill effects of so much new wealth. "Are we going to kill the golden goose by feeding the animal until its liver becomes distended and we produce a pâté which is so rich that none of us can digest it anymore? What price glory?" She told a reporter that Aspen had "become a town of glitz and glamour . . . a nut with-out a kernel." "My heart," she said, "is broken."

And that was only the beginning. The dazzle of the 1980s turned into the dot-com craze of the 1990s, which snowballed into the real estate and finance boom of the 2000s. Aspen became one of the richest towns in America, with a high concentration of billionaires, celebrities, CEOs, and Wall Streeters. Ironically, it was Aspen's anti-establishment culture and artsiness that be-came a big draw for the America's new plutocracy. There was also, of course, the appeal of other rich people, or what F. Scott Fitzgerald called in *The Great Gatsby* "the consoling proximity of millionaires."

Aspen has always been a protected place for the wealthy, surrounded by steep mountains and national forestland. Yet by the turn of the twenty-first century, the rich had blanketed the town like an overnight blizzard. Aspen's airport became a crowded parking lot of Gulfstreams, Lears, and Citations. One winter afternoon in 2006, the airport had to divert 150 jets because it was so jammed for space.

Many of the town's mom-and-pop shops shut down, unable to afford the rents. They were replaced with luxury stores owned by global giants such as Louis Vuitton, Gucci, and Prada. Knit sweaters and ski boots were out. Crocodile-skin handbags, fitted gowns, and diamonds were in. By 2008, Aspen had more than five stores selling fur coats, but only one drugstore (which also sells wine, liquor, and other high-margin goods to stay in business). The town's last toy store shut down in 2010

Its last bookstore—Explore Booksellers—almost closed in 2007 before a last-minute rescue by billionaire Sam Wyly. Wyly, a conservative Texas financier, marked a stark contrast to the store's former owner, a left-wing activist and book lover named Katherine Thalberg. Before her death in 2006, Thalberg railed against the rich, held anti-fur rallies, and raised money for Ralph Nader. Although Wyly, a book lover and writer himself, no doubt saved the store, some longtime locals criticized the purchase as yet another takeover by the right-wing rich. The *Aspen Daily News*, in its April Fool's issue, lampooned the new ownership with a fake story about Ann Coulter appearing at the store to christen the "Ann Coulter Room."

Aspen's famously egalitarian social scene became highly exclusive. The casual house parties where construction guys mixed with heiresses were replaced by private dinners in the stone mansions of Red Mountain. Private social clubs such as the Caribou Club and the ultra-lite Aspen Mountain Club allowed the wealthy to keep the right company without bumping into the hoi polloi. Tightly guarded gated communities such as Starwood became the most desired enclaves.

The most dramatic change was in real estate. By the mid-2000s, the business of Aspen was no longer tourism and skiing. It was selling homes of ever-increasing size and value to ever-wealthier buyers. In 2006, $2.6 billion worth of homes were sold in Pitkin County, which includes Aspen. The biggest sale was the $47 million purchase of Crystal Island Ranch, an estate with multiple building sites. By 2008, the median price for a single-family home in Aspen hit $5.8 million, among the highest in the country.

Saudi prince Bandar bin Sultan owned what most agreed was the most lavish spread in town—a six-property compound in Starwood that included a 56,000-square-foot main house, Hala Ranch, that has fifteen bedrooms, a spa, a beauty salon, an indoor pool, and 234 phone lines. The house was put on the market in 2006 for $135 million, a record at the time.

"This market got crazy, and I mean crazy," said Joshua Saslove, a real estate agent and the king of the mega-mansion market in Aspen. "It was like the prices were set by two guys in a room smoking a joint, and one guy would say, 'What do you think it's worth?' and the other guy would say 'How about $10 million?' And the one guy would laugh and say, 'Good one. Hey, how 'bout like $20 million!' And they would just keep going."

Even with the hallucinatory prices, demand was so strong that real estate agents could barely keep up with the buyers. "We were order takers," says Joshua. "All we did was take orders for twenty years."

There is no question that the wealth improved many aspects of Aspen life. The Aspen Institute, now run by former *Time* editor and author Walter Isaacson, has become a global powerhouse of high-minded conferences, panels, and leadership seminars.

Its board is filled with entrepreneurs, Wall Streeters, and former CEOs, and its annual summer Ideas Festival has become a kind of Davos West, featuring the likes of Alan Greenspan, Madeleine Albright, and Bill Gates.

The Aspen Santa Fe Ballet, the Aspen Music Festival, Theatre Aspen, and Jazz Aspen have all become famous far beyond the town's borders. While the ski season used to be the main draw, Aspen is now filled throughout the year with concerts, art exhibits, craft fairs, book readings, poetry contests, and food fests. Summer is now its busiest season.

The Aspen Art Museum, with funding from a new crowd of New York and L.A. collectors, is planning to move out of its current home in an old hydropower plant and into a shiny new 37,000-square-foot modernist building downtown.

"The wealthy have done a lot for Aspen." says John Phelan, an affable New York hedge fund manager who, with his wife, Amy, is a major donor to the Aspen Art Museum. "They've done more than people realize."

Aspen's $43 million high school, one of the nicest in the state of Colorado, has also received property-tax dollars from the wealthy. The town has more than 250 nonprofits—from animal shelters to the hugely successful Aspen Buddy Program, which pairs mentors with disadvantaged youth—supported in large party by the alms of the rich.

Yet even the wealthy agree that the big money of the past twenty years has had some downsides. Aside from the usual side effects of gentrification—including social dislocations, class stratification, and $5 muffins—Aspen highlights a deeper problem. Rather than insulating the town from downturns, an influx of high-beta wealth may have made Aspen more economically unstable.

TROPHY HOUSES, TROPHY WIVES

On New Year's Day in 2010, folk singer Dan Sheridan was playing his usual gig at Sneaky's Tavern, just outside of Aspen. With his baseball cap, button-down shirt, and guitar, Dan had become one of the unofficial balladeers of the laid-back mountain crowd.

He moved to Aspen in 1988, after a ski-bum friend suggested he come visit. Dan arrived with nothing but his guitar and a black trash bag filled with his clothes. He instantly fell in love with the town and the hiking, cycling, fishing, and jogging in the surrounding mountains. He got a job bagging groceries and slept on his friend's couch.

Over time, Dan pulled together enough music gigs to make a living. He got married, had two kids, and was lucky enough to win the "lottery" to buy an affordable trailer in town. At forty-four years old, with soft blue eyes, a receding hairline, and scruffy chin, Dan has the weather-beaten cheeriness of many longtime resort workers.

For the past twenty years, he has carried his guitar from bar to bar, providing comfortable background music to skiers and tourists as they warmed up after a day on the slopes. He sang Jackson Browne, Paul Simon, and James Taylor covers, along with his own tunes. He wrote about the bucolic Rocky Mountain life, about the cold, clear streams and the warm people. On that New Year's Day in 2010, Sneaky's Tavern was packed, since it was peak season. Dan was winding down his act. He had performed many of his standards, including "Small Town Love," "Be the Light," and "All This Beauty." Then he sang a song that was fast becoming a local favorite. It was called "Big Money Ruins Everything."

I was walking my dog, down the old walking trail,
When I ran into a posted sign, "Pending Future Sale"
To some Hollywood mogul, who feels that he should
Build a mansion in the mountains, his "cabin in the woods"

They come here from Miami, they come here from L.A.
And bring a part of a city that will never go away
Like a fear of strangers, accelerated time
The sound of car alarms, in a town without crime
Like quaint wooden fences, patrolled security
Setting up borders where they never used to be

Down in their graves you can hear the miners sing
Big money ruins everything

Well, it happened in Aspen, and down in Santa Fe
It happens everywhere, when the locals move away
Because we can't afford to live here, we can't afford the rent
Unless we win the lottery, or live in a tent

I think big money sucks, please write that down
Please take a look what it did to this town
Trophy houses, trophy wives,
Trophy people leading trophy lives

Down in their graves you can hear the miners sing
Big money ruins everything

Say goodbye to all the artists, and people who can ski
Say hello to private golf courses and elective surgery
I think I'll build a billboard at the entrance of this town
If you came to prove how rich you are, please just turn around

———

Please turn around, hightail and run
You probably already ruined where you coming from

So I went to the hardware store, but it has been replaced
With a boutique for trophy wives, with a reconstructed face
All it sells is handbags, stuff you'll never need
Like fine Italian shoes, or tasteful jewelry
So we blame it on the landlords, blame it all on greed
We blame it on the excess, of the nouveau riche

Down in their graves you can hear the miners sing
Big money ruins everything

The crowd cheered and laughed. They loved it, which always struck Dan as a little strange, since many of his listeners—wearing shearling coats and custom-made cowboy boots—were the very people he was writing about. He wrapped up the gig with a rousing version of "The Itsy Bitsy Spider" for a group of four-year-olds. Then he went home.

The next day he got a call from Aspen Ski Co., which owned Sneaky's. A company vice president had been in the audience during the New Year's Day performance of "Big Money Ruins Everything," and apparently he wasn't amused.

Dan was fired and asked not to play at any other Aspen Ski Co. venues. "Our job is to welcome these visitors to town, not to promote class warfare," Ski Co.'s spokesman Jeff Hanle told the *Denver Post*.

Dan was stunned. He had never thought of himself as a class warrior—just a folk singer from Fredonia, New York, who liked to play for tourists. "Big Money Ruins Everything" was supposed to be funny. At least that's what he thought.

After he was fired, Dan wasn't sure how he was going to make a living. Aspen Ski Co. owned most of the bars and restaurants where he played. Without any income during the peak tourist season, he wouldn't be able to pay his bills. "I was pretty bummed," he said.

The next day, word of Dan's firing quickly spread through town. Many of the longtime locals had had enough of the big-money crowd throwing their weight around and bullying people with their wealth. They were furious at Aspen Ski Co. The company's firing of a folk singer, while it may have been trivial in the scheme of Aspen life, became a flashpoint for Aspen's economic war between the rich and the longtime locals.

The *Aspen Times* wrote an article on Dan's firing, which unleashed a flood of letters to the editor. Dan was barraged with supportive phone calls, letters, and e-mails. Denver TV stations and radio stations came to interview him. His church congregation burst into applause at Sunday services. Some Aspenites called for a boycott of Aspen Ski Co. to protest what they saw as a heavy-handed attempt to silence any criticism of the wealthy.

After mounting publicity, Aspen Ski Co. backed down. A company spokesman announced, "The Ski Company acted hastily, made a mistake and is now acting to repair that mistake." He added that "the way it was handled was not proper" and didn't match the company's values.

The Aspen Ski Co. told Dan he could play at their bars and restaurants anytime—as long as he didn't play "Big Money Ruins Everything." Dan declined. By then, he had plenty of other gigs from all the publicity. And he didn't want to work for a company that was so fiercely protective of the wealthy and their interests.

"If they want to be on the side of the Madoff crowd, on the side of all those people who have building contests to show how rich they are and who ruin all the open space and the mountains, well, good for them. I'd rather not be on that side."

Until 2010, Dan had never even realized he had a "side." He loved Aspen and most of the people who lived there. He's always sought out the good in people, whether they had money or not. Some of his best friends are wealthy, he says. Yet he feels most comfortable with the people usually referred to in Aspen as "the worker bees"—the bartenders, waiters, cleaning ladies, musicians, writers, and artists who keep the place running every day as the super-rich blow in and out.

Dan didn't see himself as a class warrior or musical activist in the Bob Dylan or Arlo Guthrie mode. He was a guy with a guitar who played fun songs for skiers. He was more in the mold of John Denver, the sunny folk singer who also lived in Aspen. As Dan tells it, "Big Money Ruins Everything" wasn't written to become the anthem for Aspen's anti-wealth crowd (though that's exactly what it became). He wrote it to tell people about a bad morning he had on the jogging trails.

"I'm a big runner, and I've always liked running out in nature, in open space. One day I was running on one of my favorite trails in the east end and I noticed that the trail had been diverted for construction. So I'm running along this detour and all of the sudden this big guy riding an ATV pulls up with his walkie-talkie. And he's very stern and he says, 'Can I help you?' So I said, 'What?' 'Can I help you?' 'Um, no, you can't help me. I'm jogging on the trail, thanks.'

"So the guy says, 'Well, you need to get off the property now. It's private property.' I could see that the trail was next to some big development for luxury homes. It used to be a jogging trail that everyone used and now this security guard was telling me that I couldn't run there anymore. I said, 'Yeah, fine, I'm going.' I was so angry that I went home and sat down and wrote the song. It was really about losing public space and nature to people who think they own it. And I guess they do."

Dan didn't play the song much at first. It wasn't one of his fa-vorites, "and I don't think my best one." But over time, audiences started asking for it every time he played. By 2010 it had become his most requested song.

"It was surprising to me," he said. "Especially since the crowds are sometimes the wealthy. They never think it's about them. They always assume it's about someone else, about the guy who's even richer with an even bigger house."

Whatever the audience, "Big Money Ruins Everything" struck a deep chord. It summed up the discontents of Aspen's longtime residents who watched their town become a Rocky Mountain wealth preserve. The song mourned Aspen's lost soul. And it shone a light on the vanity and bling of the new rich, who clearly had their own version of the Paepckes' "Aspen idea."

"We have an economic war going on," Helen Klanderud, As-pen's former mayor, told me at the Gatsby party. "There are a lot of people who would like Aspen to be like the 1970s again. Those were glorious times here. But that's gone. To those people, if you've got money, you're bad."

Yet beyond the stereotypes and the typical complaints about high prices, "Big Money Ruins Everything" also spoke to a deeper fear among the town's leaders. It was a fear that traced back to those old silver miners singing from their graves, telling the story of how they paraded their own giant nuggets of wealth through Aspen's streets, only to see it all come crashing down years later.

It was a fear that big money could ruin everything, but in a way that was different from the hyper-gentrification described in Dan's song. Rather than providing Aspen with economic stability, high-beta wealth may have made the town more prone to booms, busts, and sudden economic dislocations.

THE TRICK-OR-TREAT INDEX

On a rainy afternoon in downtown Aspen, Mayor Mick Ireland is helping to host Aspen's first Blues and Barbecue Weekend. The streets are lined with dozens of smoke pits cooking slabs of ribs, loins, and pork butts. For less than $10, visitors can get a paper plate piled high with pulled pork, a Coke, and two slices of white bread. They also get a free blues concert on the outdoor stage, set at the foot of Aspen Mountain. Despite the downpour, hundreds of families sit on bales of hay or dance in the mud to the music.

"This is what we're trying to build more of in Aspen," says Mayor Ireland, a lanky attorney in a T-shirt and cargo shorts, who first came to Aspen as a dishwasher and busboy. "We're trying to let people know that they can come to Aspen even if they're not super rich."

Mick Ireland's message marks a dramatic turnaround from the Aspen of the past two decades. Throughout the 1990s and 2000s, Aspen pinned its hopes on the wealthy. It kept property taxes low, so the rich would come and build bigger, more expensive homes. The hotels, shops, and restaurants raised prices so high that the town became unaffordable for all but the elite. Rooms at the Little Nell start at $500 a night during ski season, and the Chilean sea bass goes for $39 a plate at Matsuhisa, run by the international sushi chef Nobu Matsuhisa.

Aspen's tax revenue no longer came from ski boots, burgers, and beer; now it was from highly discretionary luxury items such as jewelry, fur coats, and handbags. "I think it became the implicit policy for a lot of businesses and nonprofits to focus on the very high end, the people with a lot of money," Ireland said. "Some people thought that you would have fewer growth problems if you had a smaller number of people spending a larger amount of money."

Their theory worked—for a while. The town's tax revenues soared, and unemployment fell to under 4 percent. Demand for labor became so high that the rich began outbidding each other for household help and maintenance crews. Construction workers would often walk off a job because a richer person down the street offered more money.

Yet by the mid-2000s, the downside of wealth dependence started becoming clear. Among the biggest problems was the huge shift in the population from full-time locals to wealthy seasonal residents.

Between 1996 and 2007, the number of permanent residents in Aspen's high-priced West End fell by more than half, even though the number of homes stayed largely the same. Aspenites call this "going dark," since the wealthy typically spend only a few weeks a year in the homes, leaving them empty and dark the rest of the year.

Michael Cleverly says the shift has hollowed out many of Aspen's most prized neighborhoods. "You go to the West End and people still have their Christmas decorations up until July 4," he says. "They're never there. Aspen is not their second home. It's their ninth or tenth home. You know those satellite pictures where they look down at the earth at night and North Korea looks like a black spot? Well, that's the West End, and now other parts of Aspen too. They're like giant black holes."

Mick Ireland calls it the "trick-or-treat indicator." A former journalist and regional planner, Ireland loves to create maps illustrating Aspen's shifting population and social trends. According to one map, a thousand new homes or housing units were added to Aspen between 1996 and 2007. Yet the number of voters declined by five hundred. "That tells me that we were converting a substantial number of full-time residences to part-time residences," he says.

His findings are confirmed every Halloween. "On Halloween, kids go where the candy is. They're very good at finding it. If you go back fifteen years or so, they used to go all over town, including the West End. Now there are no trick-or-treaters in the West End on Halloween. Why? Because there's no candy there. The houses are dark."

All those empty homes paying taxes might sound like a mayor's dream. Seasonal residences generate revenues but use few services. Yet the extreme nature of Aspen's wealth created a new set of problems.

As the seasonal homes for the rich grew in size, they needed ever larger staffs to maintain them—even when the owners were gone. One local politician described them as "cruise ships on land," with their attendant armies of cleaning people, groundskeepers, plumbers, electricians, woodworkers, wine stewards, art caretakers, and window washers.

Very few if any of those caretakers can afford to live in Aspen. So they have to commute from Basalt, Carbondale, or other towns more than fifteen miles away. All those workers driving in to town have created monumental traffic jams every morning, not to mention strains on other services such as law enforcement and health care. In Pitkin County, which includes Aspen, the percentage of the local workforce housed within the county fell from about 73 percent in 1985 to less than 40 percent, meaning that the county was increasingly reliant on imported labor.

"It's a strange paradox," Mayor Ireland says. "The more empty homes we have, the more workers we need to maintain them. Since there aren't locals to fill the jobs, the labor comes from outside. And that creates traffic and all sorts of problems. The jobs may be growing here, but the population of people who can fill them is declining."

The combination of more dark homes and more imported labor has created an increasingly transient community. Neither the wealthy nor their help really live in Aspen, yet they make up a large share of the economy. Just as the wealth boom and rising riches of the wealthy seems to be hollowing out the American middle class, it's also leaving large holes in high-end communities.

On the surface, Aspen weathered the financial crisis and Great Recession better than most towns. Its unemployment rate in 2010 held steady at around 7 percent—less than the nation's 9.6 percent. Its median home price has held fast at around $6 million. Aspen is unquestionably still a very rich town.

But behind the affluent exterior, Aspen's economy is struggling to find a sustainable future. And high-beta wealth has made Aspen's ups and downs more extreme.

The hotels and stores that once touted ever-higher prices are now struggling with big demand swings. The Jerome Hotel, which famously hosted Elizabeth Paepcke during her first trip to town, became entangled in the Lehman Brothers bankruptcy because of a loan from the investment bank. The hotel filed for bankruptcy and was purchased by Chicago investors for a fraction of the amount offered for the hotel before the financial crisis.

The St. Regis Aspen, after suffering a decline in occupancy, was sold in 2010 to an unknown Delaware-based buyer. The shopping area downtown is now pocked with empty storefronts and For Lease signs.

Some of Aspen's most prominent names suffered losses to their fortunes and reputations. The Bucksbaum family, the Chicago-based clan that controlled the nation's second-largest shopping mall empire, lost more than two-thirds of its net worth between 2008 and 2009. The family's company, called General Growth

Properties, filed for bankruptcy protection because of its crushing debt load. The family's stock, once worth more than $6 billion, shrank to a mere $25 million, though it eventually gained back some ground.

The Bucksbaums are among Aspen's largest philanthropists, giving to the Aspen Music Festival, the Aspen Institute, the ballet, and other cultural institutions. While the arts groups declined to comment on the family's giving, several town officials and arts patrons said some branches of the Bucksbaum family had dramatically cut back their giving.

Sam Wyly, the Dallas billionaire who bought the local Explore Booksellers, and his late brother, Charles, gave generously to local charities. Both came under fire in 2009 for alleged tax fraud. A lawsuit filed by the Securities and Exchange Commission alleges that the Wylys used secret offshore accounts to hide stock sales and other assets. The Wylys have denied the charges.

Bernie Madoff also reached into Aspen's pocket. While Palm Beach and New York got most of the attention, Aspen had dozens of Madoff investors who lost their life savings. Some news accounts put the losses in Aspen at more than $1 billion. Lenny "Boogie" Weinglass, a longtime Aspen businessman who owns Boogie's Diner and a large clothing store in town, said most of the rich people he knows in Aspen have lost at least 25 percent to 30 percent of their wealth since 2008. "A lot of my bigwig friends got hurt bad this time around," he said. "I know at least a dozen people who lost everything with Madoff. I know, let's see, maybe six or seven people who were worth more than $100 million who are now worth maybe $10 million. And I know a whole lot of guys who lost 30 to 40 percent in investments or real estate. They're quiet about it, and they like to keep a stiff upper lip in public. But lots of people in this town lost a lot of money."

One morning I took a drive with Joshua Saslove, the Aspen

real estate broker who helped pioneer the market for $20 million homes in town. When there's a trophy property in Aspen for sale, Joshua is usually the one selling it. I asked him to take me to some of his most expensive listings. But rather than a tour of Aspen's rich and famous, I got a tour of fallen fortunes.

First we went to a 7,500-square-foot mansion festooned with intricate wood carvings, digitally controlled window shades, countless flat-panel TV screens, and stained glass. The house also had two "safe rooms"—a dressing room and a bathroom—that became bombproof shelters when the doors were locked.

Joshua politely refused to talk about the owner. But I later found out he was a dot-com tycoon who had made hundreds of millions of dollars after selling his company. He and his wife had made large pledges to charity, and they were now struggling to honor their commitments in the wake of investment losses. They had spent more than $30 million to build the house, but it was listed for $16 million. And it still hadn't attracted buyers.

In the downstairs media room stood a memory of better times—a life-size cardboard cutout of the couple, smiling and dressed for a black-tie ball. Their photos had been pasted onto a six-foot-tall piece of cardboard and propped up with a stand. Joshua stood in front of the couple and smiled. "They looked pretty happy back then, huh?"

Next we toured a 14,000-square-foot stone mansion that was part royal château and part dude ranch. The heated driveway led to an arched portico with a twenty-foot-high wooden door. The interior was filled with deer-antler chandeliers, Italianate fireplaces, onyx bathtubs, and giant flat-screen TVs. Along with the wine cellar, home theater, and gym, the property also had a guesthouse and a horse stable, which doubled as a ballroom and party house. Records show the owner is also a tech tycoon who,

Joshua says without being specific, "had undergone some financial changes."

Of course, real estate and personal wealth fell everywhere between 2008 and 2010. But Aspen's losses, and the impact on its economy, were more dramatic because of its dependence on the high-betas.

Real estate sales fell by more than 65 percent between 2007 and 2009. That compares with the national sales-price declines of about 45 percent. Aspen's median sales price spiraled from $5.8 million to $1.6 million—far greater than the national decline of 40 percent. Aspen's consumer economy, relying as it did on people's ongoing need for Gucci shades and tuna belly, also collapsed. Its sales tax receipts fell by more than 15 percent between April 2008 and April 2010—nearly three times the decline reported by Vail and other nearby ski resorts. The luxury bust left more than a dozen stores closed and one of America's most expensive streets with empty windows.

At the same time, rents have not fallen far enough to lure back the drugstores, grocery stores, and mom-and-pop shops that can sell more everyday items.

"It's kind of the worst of both worlds," said one downtown retailer. "We got a town for the rich, but the rich aren't spending. It's not like other towns, where you have a middle class that needs to keep buying milk and bread and underwear every day. People don't need to buy $20,000 watches. In Aspen it's like someone just shut the water off."

Local charities have also taken a hit. When local nonprofits depended on small donations from large numbers of people, they could ride out the economic cycles. Now that many nonprofits have bet their futures on a select few rich backers, some of whom stopped giving, they are scrambling to survive.

"There are quite a few people who are now avoiding my calls," says Boogie Weinglass. "I tell them it's okay to just give a little. But they just don't want to have the conversation."

Mayor Mick Ireland says the wealth shocks in Aspen have forced a radical change in thinking. Rather than being a mega-mall for millionaires, the town has to become a playground for the people, or at least the merely affluent. It has to figure out a way to lower the prices of housing, hotel rooms, restaurants, ski lift tickets, and just about everything else in town—a feat that many say is impossible. Yet the mayor says that reducing Aspen's dependence on a small group of itinerant rich people is the only way the town will preserve its culture and its past.

On the same afternoon that the Gatsby party is winding down, with many attendees headed for supper at the Little Nell, the Big Aspen BBQ Block Party is in full swing. Hundreds of people are lined up for $5 lime pork tacos and Tennessee ribs slathered in sauce. The Otis Taylor Band is belting out its own brand of "trance blues" to hundreds of fans and kids dancing in the mud and rain.

The mayor, who helped create the festival, rides his bike through the crowds and chats with some of the longtime locals. He says the festival is a taste of the new Aspen, a town that draws families of all incomes and ages, and celebrates a history of arts and culture rather than wealth and status. He's not sure how to get prices down at the hotels and restaurants. But at least, on this afternoon, visitors can get a $5 lunch.

"You don't see many rich guys here," he says excitedly. "In fact, lots of the people here are people I've never seen, they're new. That tells me it was a successful event.

When I ask about whether it brings in more money and jobs than events like the Gatsby party, he laughs. "Things like the

Gatsby party are great. We need those. But the block party tells me that you don't have to be rich to have a good time in Aspen."

By the spring of 2011, Aspen's crisis seemed to be melting away like another winter's snowfall, making way for another boom cycle to pop up from the empty shops and For Sale signs on East Main Street. Housing prices were once again smashing records. The *Wall Street Journal* named it the most expensive town in America, noting that Aspen had "formed its own orbit," with the lowest-priced home in town—located in a trailer park—listed for $559,000.

Yet Aspen's next crisis—and there will be a next crisis—will likely be even more extreme than the last. More than two hundred years after the silver bust almost wiped Aspen off the map, the town is once again home to a financial mania, this time from stock markets and asset bubbles rather than silver prices. It will never suffer another 1890s catastrophe. But hypercycles of euphoria and despair, and the strains they produce on the daily bonds of community, are now as much a feature of Aspen's landscape as the snowcapped peak of Mount Sopris.

It's not just towns like Aspen that are experiencing the sudden drops of high-beta wealth. It's also the people and companies that serve the wealthy.

7

—————

GIVING JEEVES THE PINK SLIP

In the run-up to the 2008 financial crisis, economists and consumer experts were sharply divided over the timing and severity of any recession. They largely were united, however, on one issue: the continued spending of the rich.

The wealthy, they wrote, had plenty of money, and would therefore keep buying. Michael Silverstein, the consumer guru and co-author of *Trading Up*, declared in 2005 that the luxury economy was "quite recession proof."

He was wrong, of course. The luxury economy rose further and fell harder than any other sector of the economy. One reason was the spikes and crashes of high-beta wealth and incomes, described in Chapter 2. Yet the other cause is a new spending pattern among the wealthy, which more closely resembles binges and crash diets than the moderate luxury spending of the postwar period.

Economists Jonathan Parker and Annette Vissing-Jorgensen used the national Consumer Expenditure Survey to get a closer look at these changes. They found the spending volatility of those

·in the top-earning 10 percent of households is ten times higher than the spending volatility of those in the bottom 80 percent of households: "The consumption of high-consumption households is more exposed to aggregate booms and busts than that of the typical household."

One survey showed that from 2007 to 2008, consumers with incomes from $150,000 to $249,000 cut their spending by about 8 percent, while those above $250,000 slashed their spending by nearly 15 percent.

Ajay Kapur, a Wall Street equity analyst who also studies the spending habits of the rich, says that the rich are far more un-predictable as consumers than the rest of the population—not because they're especially frugal during bad times, but because they're so euphoric during good times, buying boats, handbags, five-star vacations, and new kitchens.

"Their spending behavior is a lot more volatile than the Aver-age Joe's," he wrote in a 2009 research note. "On the way up and down, their behavior is considerably more bouncy than the over-all economy."

Consider the chart on page 154. The dark line represents the ROB ETF, a basket of stocks representing companies that sell to the wealthy—from Porsche and BMW to Sotheby's, Wilmington Trust, Bulgari, and LVMH. It's a kind of Richistan Index, repre-senting the consumer economy of the wealthy.

The gray line is a basket of stocks for mainstream U.S. retailers and consumer companies—everything from Walmart and Home Depot to Gap and Macy's. It's more like a Main Street Index.

The Main Street Index is fairly stable, like a flat midwestern plain with a lone mountain in the middle. The Richistan Index is more like the Rocky Mountains, with steep drops and moun-tain peaks. Main Street has a low beta. Richistan's spending has a high beta.

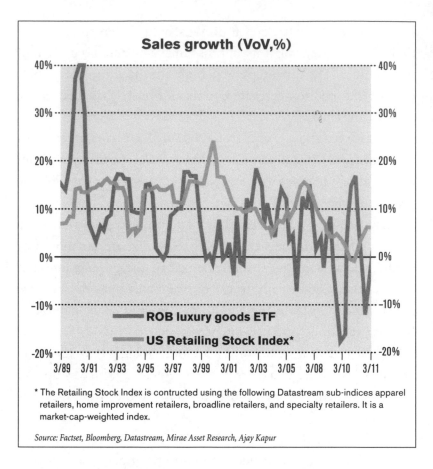

Sales growth (VoV,%)

* The Retailing Stock Index is contructed using the following Datastream sub-indices apparel retailers, home improvement retailers, broadline retailers, and specialty retailers. It is a market-cap-weighted index.

Source: Factset, Bloomberg, Datastream, Mirae Asset Research, Ajay Kapur

Kapur explains, "Average Americans spend a lot of their incomes on necessities, things like toothpaste or broccoli or shaving cream. Even if they have to tighten their budgets, they're still going to buy toothpaste and broccoli. For the wealthy, many of their purchases are discretionary. So if they have a bad bonus, they're not going to buy a luxury item."

To illustrate this further, the chart on page 155 shows the prices and sales volumes of the Gulfstream V, one of the most prestigious and pricey private jets. Average prices soared in the late 1990s during the dot-com boom to more than $40 million. Then they crashed by more than 20 percent in the early 2000s.

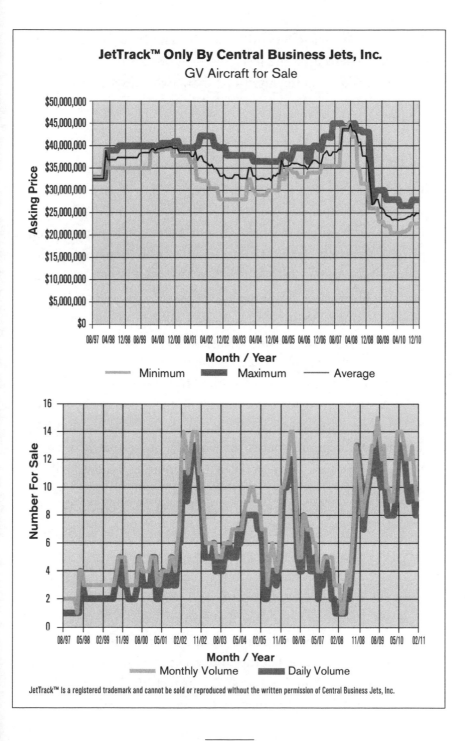

JetTrack™ Only By Central Business Jets, Inc.
GV Aircraft for Sale

JetTrack™ Is a registered trademark and cannot be sold or reproduced without the written permission of Central Business Jets, Inc.

They rocketed back to $45 million in the late 2000s before falling by about 50 percent in the recession of 2008–2010. Sales volumes are even spikier, falling by more than two-thirds in the early 2000s, and by more than 90 percent in 2008.

Private jets, which many assume to be well insulated from economic ups and downs, have become even more volatile than everyday passenger cars. The same patterns emerge for boats, Bentleys, yachts, Swiss watches, racehorses, and other luxury goods. When times are good for the rich, prices and demand explode. When financial markets crash or asset bubbles pop, the rich virtually stop buying. As Michael Repole, the billionaire founder of VitaminWater and an avid buyer of Thoroughbred horses, told me: "No one needs a racehorse."

Does anyone really notice if the rich buy a mountain of Manolo Blahniks and Bentleys one year and none the next?

Increasingly they do. In 2005, Kapur was working as an equity strategist at Citigroup and wanted to figure out why rising oil prices weren't having a greater impact on the consumer economy. He came up with a theory of what he called "the plutonomy," economies—including that of the United States—that were dominated by spending by the wealthy. Plutonomies behaved differently than did economies dominated by a middle class. While high oil and gas prices may have crimped spending for the middle class, they mattered less to a plutonomy, since wealthy consumers weren't as affected by higher gas prices.

"There are rich consumers, few in number but disproportionate in the gigantic slice of income and consumption they take," he wrote. "There are the rest, the 'non-rich,' the multitudinous many, but only accounting for surprisingly small bites of the national pie." This meant that the companies serving the rich would prosper far more than those serving "the rest" during expansions. The old adage "Sell to the masses, live with the classes" had been turned on its head. The new way to prosperity was to "sell to the classes."

Even Kapur, however, didn't realize however extreme the plutonomy would become. In his first research notes, Ajay projected that the top 20 percent of Americans by income accounted for up to half of all consumer spending. By 2010, research showed that America's consumer spending had become even more highly concentrated at the top. Mark Zandi, the chief economist for Moody's Analytics, found that the top-earning 5 percent of American households accounted for 37 percent of all consumer outlays (outlays include consumer spending, interest payments on installment debt, and transfer payments).

By contrast, the bottom 80 percent of Americans account for 39.5 percent of all consumer outlays. In other words, the few million Americans at the top of the income ladder spend about as much as the hundreds of millions at the bottom.

Zandi also determined that the dominance of the rich was a fairly recent phenomenon. In 1990, the top 5 percent accounted for 25 percent of consumer outlays. Their share held relatively steady until the mid-1990s, when it started inching up past 30 percent. After the bull market of the 2000s, it reached its all-time record. The upstairs-downstairs nature of the recovery in 2010 and 2011, in which the rich rebounded, further boosted the top 5 percent's share of spending.

As Michael Feroli, chief U.S. economist at JPMorgan Chase, wrote: "The heavy lifting is being done by the upper-income households"—if one defines a Birkin bag as heavy, of course.

We know, then, that the wealthy have become the dominant spenders in the U.S. consumer economy, which itself accounts for two-thirds of the GDP. And we also know that the spending of the wealthy has become more manic due to their fast-changing fortunes and frivolous splurges during booms.

The result is a U.S. consumer economy that will increasingly resemble the Richistan Index. And since more and more of the service economy is devoted to the wealthy, jobs will also move in line with the fortunes of the rich. To understand the human costs of high-beta wealth and the changing nature of working for the rich, consider the plight of the modern butler.

BUTLER OF THE YEAR

Every year, butlers from across America gather for their annual convention. As conventions go, it is a highly practical and well-mannered affair. The butlers attend panels called "Forming Boundaries with Our Employer" and "Legal Rights of Household Staff," as well as workshops on smart-home technology, fur coat care, and silver polishing. In between sessions, they eagerly serve each other coffee and tea and trade business cards.

On their final night, the butlers break out the champagne to raise a toast to the Outstanding Private Service Manager, also known as Butler of the Year. The award is like the Oscar of butlering. It's given to the butler who displays the best traits and traditions of butlerhood—loyalty, hard work, discretion, expert judgment, leadership, and that most elusive but important butler quality known as the "service heart."

Butlers, by nature and profession, shy away from attention, even in their awards. But in 2007 I was invited to the Denver Sheraton to present the Butler of the Year award.

For me, butlers held a peculiar fascination. They were figures from another era in wealth—the fabled Jeeves with his silver tray, upturned nose, and tux—yet they had managed to transform themselves for the new age of riches. Butlers were now the crisis managers for the newly rich McMansion set. Butlers had their own management training, org charts, spreadsheets, and bud-gets. They even had their own software to run the increasingly complex lives and homes of the rich, solidifying their image as butlers for the digital age—Jeeves 2.0.

Butlers weren't even called butlers anymore. They now pre-fer the title of household manager or estate manager. And they demand salaries commensurate with their training and surging demand for their services: $60,000 to $200,000 a year, depending on experience.

When I first wrote about the remaking of the modern butler in Richistan, to me the butler was a symbol of all that had changed about American wealth, including the changing habits and values of the new rich, who now wanted workaholic, tech-savvy manag-ers rather than the silver-tray-holding house mascots of yore.

I even spent a few days at butler boot camp, a butler train-ing school better known as the Starkey International Institute for Household Management. I learned how to iron a shirt, how to pack a suitcase for a private jet in under five minutes, and how to divide a 30,000-square-foot mansion into zones for cleaning and security checks. I tried my hand at the "ballet of service," where a team of butlers serves a meal in precise synchronization (I was politely dismissed after nearly dropping a salad plate).

"We are not servants anymore," said Mary Starkey, Starkey In-ternational's owner and founder. "We are now professionals."

The winner that year was Curtis Laurent, a dapper and soft-spoken butler from New Orleans. Laurent had grown up in a poor family in New Orleans, and in his early twenties he found work as a chauffeur for a rich banking family in town. He earned the family's trust and attended Starkey to get his household manage-ment degree.

Laurent couldn't read or write when he got to Starkey. Since he had all the other makings of a great butler, they got him a tutor, and he wound up graduating at the top of his class. He returned to his employer in New Orleans and was promoted to estate manager, responsible for running their four homes and household staff of seven.

Soon after, New Orleans was devastated by Hurricane Katrina. Laurent's employer evacuated before the storm, but Laurent stayed on and guarded their mansion. During the floods, the home filled with three feet of water, and Laurent saved the valuables—furniture, artwork, rugs—by carrying them upstairs. He stayed awake for days looking out for looters or vandals.

Laurent has what butlers call "the service heart"—an undying dedication to making other people happy and giving them what they need. His idea of service even extended to the community of New Orleans. In the months after Katrina, he launched a charity drive to buy school uniforms and school supplies for underprivileged kids. He also coached Little League and contributed time and money to inner-city youth programs.

"I'm trying to do what I can to help New Orleans move on and improve," he said to the audience after I handed him his shiny red plaque. "Service to me isn't just about my job. It's also about serving my community."

I called Laurent three years after giving him the award to see how he was doing. Butlers had become something of a barometer of the wealth boom, reflecting both the spending and habits of the newly rich. I wondered what the barometer would tell me about the bust.

Laurent answered the phone with his usual hyperpoliteness.

"Yes, Mr. Frank. So very nice to hear from you. What can I do for you, sir?"

We chatted for a few minutes before I asked him about his job situation. "Oh, I'm doing all right," he said. "Everything's good, real good." As we talked, however, it became clear that everything wasn't real good after all.

Curtis was vague on the details, since butlers are bound by strict confidentiality clauses in their contracts. But he said that if I wanted to know how the butler economy was doing, I should contact his cousin, Anthony Harris. Anthony used to work for Curtis, before Curtis had to fire him.

"Anthony was a great butler," Laurent said. "He was about to get another promotion." He paused. "But it's a different world now for folks like us."

I take Laurent's suggestion and go to visit his cousin on a snowy February afternoon in a suburb of Washington, D.C. Anthony Harris was in the kitchen slicing a chicken timbale with truffles and placing the warm white discs onto a bed of arugula. He was wearing a crisply ironed dress shirt, jeans, and loafers. He was fit and cheerful, with a broad white smile and a palpable eagerness to please.

"Here is course number four," he says, setting down the timbale and greens. "We have a total of six courses today, so forgive me if I have to keep going back to the kitchen."

Under any circumstances, Harris's six-course culinary extravaganza would have been impressive. For the first course, he made figs infused with port wine and stuffed with mascarpone. He made ham and cheese muffalettas, followed by his famous "three-fowl" gumbo, using turkey, chicken, and duck. After the timbale came short ribs slow-cooked for three days and graced with braised Brussels sprouts and oven-roasted potatoes—all carefully paired with wines. He capped it all off with brandy and pepper crème brûlée topped with a burnt-orange glaze.

What made the meal most unusual, however, was the circumstances of its chef. Harris had been unemployed for more than four months. He was staying at his brother's house in Montclair, Maryland, and living off $400 a week in unemployment checks. He barely had enough money for gas and cell phone bills. Yet he had just prepared a meal fit for a king—or at least a hungry journalist. "The one thing my employer used to tell me is, 'Harris, you've never cooked a bad meal.'"

Harris is unceasingly optimistic. A girlfriend once broke up with him because he was so happy all the time. His co-workers at a previous job nicknamed him "No Complaints," because when they asked how he was doing, he would always say, "No Complaints!" with a beaming smile. He still carries something of the stage presence he gained from years of singing in a popular boy band in New Orleans. "With me, the glass is always half full," he says. "I'm always trying to find a solution."

Harris's true talent, however, is food. He was born to cook. His family is Cajun and Creole, and they own a catering company in New Orleans. Harris spent much of his boyhood in the kitchen with his grandmother, who founded the company. She was legendary for her gumbos, muffalettas, and beignets. From her tiny kitchen, she would cook dinners for three hundred to five hundred people, and her giant cooking pots became characters in Harris's life, with names like "The Kingpin" and "The Fooler." Harris spent weekends and nights working at the catering company, making deliveries, cleaning up, or helping out in the kitchen with his six brothers and sisters and army of cousins.

He enjoyed his glimpses into the world of wealth. When he was ten, he visited a mansion on St. Charles Street that was unlike anything he'd ever seen before. "We were doing a delivery around Christmas," he says. "It was this beautiful mansion, really old, with these Louis XIV chairs and antiques and crown moldings and beautiful art. When we walked inside, the whole house was lit up, these white Christmas lights and candles. They had pine garlands everywhere and a big tree. What I remember was the smell. That pine smell was amazing. And with the lights and the house, it was just beautiful to me."

Food, however, was his first love. He worked in more than a dozen restaurants and hotels in New Orleans, starting at a Pizza Hut and working his way up to the Ritz Carlton as a sous chef, doorman, and concierge.

His dream was to start a restaurant or become a celebrity chef. He sought out the top chefs in New Orleans and offered to chop onions or do dishes for free just so he could be in their kitchens and learn. Eventually he became proficient at cooking everything from French stews to Italian pastas, Asian fusion salads to chocolate bread pudding.

His signature dish is his gumbo. For Harris, gumbo is more than just a dish; it's a symbol of his identity, his efforts to both build on his family's history and forge his own path. "No gumbo ever tastes the same," he said. "It's different every time, even if it's made by the same person. With my gumbo, I started with the recipe from my grandmother, and I added my own thing, my own flavors. It took me years and years to get where I am with my gumbo."

In 2007, Harris was helping the family catering business with a party hosted by one of New Orleans's wealthiest families. The family's household manager, who turned out to be Curtis Laurent, was impressed with how well Harris worked the kitchen and dealt with the guests. He offered him Harris a job as the house butler.

He started work in the home of one of New Orleans's wealthiest and most powerful families. His starting pay was $40,000 a year.

He enjoyed working with Laurent and the other five members of the house staff—including the chef, who was initially testy about having another cook in the house. Harris's job was to run errands, handle the family's travel needs, and serve meals. He also acted as the advance team for the family's four vacation homes, stocking them with food and supplies before their visits. He loaded up their private jet and helicopter before trips and sometimes filled in for the gardeners, housekeepers, and chef.

After five months, he was promoted to house assistant, making $60,000 a year but often working sixty-hour weeks.

Harris couldn't divulge the name of his employer, a husband and wife. Like Laurent, he praised their generosity and kindness. Yet he also found their rarefied life somewhat puzzling. The couple lived alone in a 12,000-square-foot home with a staff of seven, "which seemed like a lot to me," he said. The couple's two grown children, who lived on their own, would often reach out to Harris to get news from home. Harris even cooked meals for the dogs—chicken soup for one, beef tips for the other.

When the financial crisis hit in 2008, Harris figured that the family and his job were safe—the rich always come out fine, he thought. Yet by the end of 2008, he had begun noticing some changes. The husband, who ran the banking business, became more brusque and stressed. He had always worked long hours, but as the financial crisis deepened, he started working on weekends, often rising before dawn. The family sold one of their vacation homes and put another on the market. They also sold the private jet.

When, in the summer of 2009, Laurent was asked to downsize his staff, he fired the chauffeur and the two groundskeepers. When Harris learned that the family was even cutting back on the regular allowances to the two kids, he knew his job was in jeopardy. "When I heard the kids were being affected, I knew there could be trouble," he said. "They were family. We were just staff."

In July 2010, Laurent called Harris into his small office and asked him to sit down. He was holding a folder filled with papers.

"I know what you're going to say," Harris said before Laurent could speak.

"How do you know?" said a surprised Laurent.

"Just stuff I've been hearing," Harris said.

Laurent handed Harris his exit papers to sign and asked if he would like to stay on as a part-time consultant without benefits. Harris thanked him, but said he'd rather try to find something full-time.

Over the next six months, Harris scoured the help-wanted ads for butlers, private chefs, and yacht cooks. He went to more than a half-dozen interviews but had no job offers. A producer in Hollywood approached him about making a reality TV show about Harris as a "food ambassador" of New Orleans. It never panned out. A placement agency in New York called him to see if he'd work with a "difficult" family on the Upper East Side that had burned through several butlers in the past year. Harris said he'd be thrilled to accept the challenge. He never got a call back.

As the days and months dragged on, Harris sat at his brother's house in Maryland. He was running out of leads. He wanted to keep working for the wealthy. But increasingly he was starting to consider other kinds of work—especially in government. His brother works in the U.S. Patent Office, and his sister works for the Labor Department in Atlanta.

"I used to think working for a wealthy family would be the most stable kind of work," he said, as we drove past the sprawling office buildings of Washington, D.C. "You know, they've got means. But now I think maybe the real job security is with the government."

Harris has plenty of company. Just as the butler boom came to symbolize the money madness of the 2000s, the butler bust illustrates the aftermath and coming era of high-beta wealth. Butlers once expected lifetime employment in the embrace of America's richest families. Now they're waking up to a lifetime of booms and busts, of rapid promotions followed by sudden firings.

Staffing experts say butler pay and employment fell more than 20 percent in 2009 and 2010 and has been slow to return. In my own sample of butlers and household manager that I've met over the years, about a third were out of work or only working part-time.

Steven Laitmon, co-founder of the Calendar Group, a Connecticut-based household staffing company, told me that rich people today are getting rid of their high-priced armies of chefs, maids, chauffeurs, gardeners, security guards, household managers, and estate managers. They still need help. Yet they're combining the jobs into one or two "super-staffers" who can do it all.

"We're getting a lot of requests from clients saying, 'What we want is someone who can do it all, from cooking and cleaning to paying the bills and watching the kids,'" said Laitmon. He noted that many clients mention Alice from the 1970s TV sitcom *The Brady Bunch*, the comical cook, housekeeper, and kid-watcher who also helped smooth over family problems. Says Laitmon: "A lot of our hedge fund clients want their own Alice."

The new all-in-one house staffer has a less exalted title and lower salary than the household managers of the boom times. The average salary for an Alice is about $60,000 to $80,000.

"What people are really looking for is a return to homespun caring and comfort," said Calendar's Nathalie Laitmon. "Alice represents a return to those values for them."

THE OCCASIONAL BUTLER

Lloyd White, a fifty-eight-year-old butler in Indiana, spent years working as the butler and assistant to a Michigan real estate billionaire. He worked hundred-hour weeks, helped run a large household staff, and traveled constantly aboard his employer's private jet. By 2010, White was unemployed and struggling to find work.

He came up with a new occupation, one more fitting to the age of high-beta wealth: occasional butler. Rather than tying his fate to a precarious plutocrat, White now rents himself out by the hour to the wealthy or merely affluent families who want someone to help them host parties or events. While he used to make $125,000 a year, now he charges $50 a hour, or about $200 for a single party, helping families with birthday parties, bar mitzvahs, and anniversaries, often helping them shop for supplies at Costco. Many of his employers are the formerly rich who used to throw more expensive parties but are now downsizing. He is the occasional help for the occasionally rich.

"It's pretty affordable. You can go to Costco and get a cheese plate, some Swedish meatballs, maybe some shrimp cocktail, and petit fours for fifty people, all for about $300," he told me. "Sure, it's a different kind of work for me. These aren't the ultra-rich. But they still like to have a nice party once in a while."

The butler slump may prove temporary, of course. Butler agencies and training schools—which have a reputation for undying optimism—said that by 2011, they were already seeing demand and salaries for butlers perk up. We may well see another boom in household staff in the next decade, with even more vaunted salaries and titles. Household CEO, perhaps?

Yet the days of lifetime employment in warm embrace of a rich family may be ending. Instead, we may be entering a new age of the occasional butler.

When Anthony Harris started butlering, he assumed that the rich were an enduring feature of our economy. He had seen them withstand recessions, political turmoil, and even the catastrophic floods of Katrina. They always landed on their feet. He figured that people like his employer had so much wealth that their lifestyles would never have to change. Since that lifestyle included butlers, Harris figured his job was among the safest in the country.

What Harris didn't realize until he was fired in 2010 is that the spending of the rich can turn on a dime, even if they still appear to be rich.

Lloyd White is another human casualty of high-beta wealth. Like Anthony Harris, he was a butler who lost his job during the recession. And like Harris, he has yet to find full-time work. While Harris still burns with excitement and eagerness to reenter the world of wealth, White is older and has the more skeptical view of a battle-scarred veteran of the butler wars. "What a lot of young people don't understand about this profession is that they'll be flying high and feeling like they're part of the family," he said. "But they're not part of the family. They are entirely expendable and there's always a day when you find that out. Usually it's within two or three years of taking the job. Some of today's wealthy don't really care about anyone but themselves. And by the way, some of them are not very good with money."

White has worked through two full cycles of high-beta wealth. In the late 1990s, he was the food-and-beverage chief at a country club. Many of the members had poured money into tech stocks. The club "was full of a lot of the very wealthy older gentlemen in town," he said. "In 2000 and 2001, they would sit in the club dining room and watch CNBC and just watch their stocks go down and down. I thought they were all going to have heart attacks. They were all losing a lot of their investments."

White moved on to work for another club, and then the Michigan billionaire. In 2009, after the billionaire's health deteriorated, he worked for two other families before being "transitioned out" of his last job in 2010.

While trying to make ends meet as an occasional butler and

by doing side work for catering companies, he holds out hope of finding another full-time butler job. "It's been a whole year since I had a family to take care of," he said, referring, of course, to a rich family that could employ him.

In the meantime, his own family has suffered. His wife is also part of the high economy built around the rich: she makes couture dresses for wealthy fashionistas. With both of their incomes crashing during the recession, the Whites defaulted on their mortgage. By 2011, the bank had foreclosed their home and was threatening to evict them. "We're kind of squatters in our own home," he says.

The Whites plan to move to Florida and patch together employment working as a butler, insurance salesperson, and manager of a website. While he's grateful for the work he had, there are two stories that stick in White's mind when he thinks about working for the new rich.

The first is from a job he had working for a family that was worth "in the hundreds of millions," he said. Every summer, White would accompany the family to their lakeside home in Canada and work as their butler for a month.

In the summer of 2010, he was driving with the mother of the family back from the house and they got to talking about money. White told her he was down to his last few thousand dollars after losing his job and most of his retirement money. The woman grew quiet, then offered a confession. "Lloyd," she said, "you know we are wealthy. But we lost an awful lot of money during the financial crisis. We lost a third of our wealth." Her eyes filled up with tears. She told White that in 2008, the family had been spending wildly and had run down their savings, so when stocks crashed in 2009, they were forced to sell some of their stocks at low prices to fund their lifestyle.

"She was literally crying the blues," White said. "I felt pretty bad. But then I'm thinking, 'Wait a minute. You're still worth like $200 million. Maybe you lost $100 million. But it's kind of hard to feel sorry for someone with $200 million.' I mean, I was down to my last $2,000 or $3,000. It's all relative. Anyway, I tried to be sympathetic."

Another family White worked for was also worth millions. During the recession, the family's income couldn't keep pace with their exuberant spending habits, which often included new Maseratis and house renovations. During a low point in the recession, one of the adult sons in the family told the house manager that if anyone was going to cut back to make ends meet, it would be the household staff.

"He said to him, 'I'm not going to be the only one to suffer because of these losses. People who work for me also have to take a hit.'" After the speech, the son fired the house chef and demanded pay cuts from all the other staffers who wanted to keep their jobs. The savings from the cuts only amounted to about $150,000 a year. As White puts it, "That's less than he spent for the new Maserati that he wrecked."

White said he was initially stunned by the remarks. It was further proof of the sense of entitlement, arrogance, and exploitativeness of the new rich, and their utter contempt for all the dim-witted plebes who weren't as rich. But White later realized the son was right. It was the little folks—the staffers, the butlers, the army of people who serve and cater to the rich—who seem to bear the brunt of the financial pain when the high-beta rich take a fall. It wasn't an opinion. It was economic fact.

"You can ride the wave and hopefully save some money and be smart with your investments along the way. You should ride that wave as long as you can. Because eventually, that wave will come crashing down."

When the waves of high-beta wealth come crashing down,

they can affect an entire town like Aspen as well as a much larger canvas like the American consumer economy. In a plutonomy, we're all occasional butlers now, relying on the increasingly erratic jobs and spending of the wealthy.

As the rich account for a growing share of taxes, the high-beta swings will also be felt in the broader realm of government. In the next chapter, we'll find out what a butler and Bentley dealer have in common with the governor of California.

8

WHAT'S WRONG WITH CALIFORNIA?

Brad Williams is a tall, lanky, and slightly awkward economist who rides his bike to work, listens to Willie Nelson on his iPod, and takes long hikes in the woods. Yet for more than twenty years, he had one of the most important jobs in California government: forecasting the state's economy, as well as its tax collections. His predictions had a profound impact. If he was right, the state had a better chance of closing the year with a balanced budget. If he was off by just a few percentage points, California could wind up with shortfalls of billions of dollars.

Most of the time he was dead right. The *Wall Street Journal* named him California's most accurate economic forecaster between 1987 and 1998, beating out economists from the state's top banks, business groups, and universities.

For his accuracy, Williams credited his deep data dives. Other California economists usually cobbled together their forecasts from standard-issue government data, which were stale by the time they came out, or from national statistics that they then would apply to California.

Williams and his team developed what he called a "structural econometric model," a computer model involving more than a hundred interdependent factors, including interest rates, salaries, and taxable sales. He constantly refreshed his forecasts with data revisions or new statistics, pulling in numbers from a wider array of sources and running them through his number crunchers.

Once all the models were run, Williams turned to his most reliable tool: his gut instinct. Behind his data-driven exterior, Williams practiced a kind of Zen forecasting, setting aside the numbers and models and meditating on an economic question. He might be sitting at his desk or riding his bike when he would arrive at a view on, say, the California housing market or the future of aerospace wages.

"I'm not beholden to data," he says. "Data and modeling can give you a structure and a way to think about a problem, but you have to broaden it. Once you look at the data and the models, you try to stand back. There's a lot of reflection. The data will tell you what impact a decline in the housing sector may have on employment or other parts of the economy. But it won't tell you whether real estate will fall or rise. That's where you use reason and judgment. It's just a lot of thinking."

In the mid-1990s, however, Williams encountered a problem that even his most intense thinking marathons and computer models couldn't solve. For decades, California's economy had moved broadly in line with its tax revenues. If the state's GDP and employment were growing strongly, so were tax revenues. When times were tough, taxes also went down.

Suddenly, however, the California economy began to split in two. Tax revenues (especially income-tax revenues) began to soar while the broader economy and wages remained flat. Williams's complex econometric models stopped working, since the usual connections and explanations no longer applied.

"It was like we suddenly had two different states," Williams said. "We had the California economy and then we had personal income taxes. The traditional economic measures of personal income and employment somehow had become less significant in explaining what was going on in the economy, especially in terms of revenue." In his more than 20 years of forecasting, he had rarely encountered such a puzzle. He and his team did months of economic sleuthing. They discovered that most of the increase in income taxes was coming from a small group of people making astronomical incomes—some in the hundreds of millions of dollars.

He also discovered that most of those super-earners lived and worked in Silicon Valley, and that most of their incomes were coming from stock sales. Using salary studies and information from the state tax department, he found that the average incomes of the top 20 percent of Californians (households making at least $95,000 in 1998) jumped by nearly 50 percent between 1993 and 1998, while incomes for the rest of the state grew by less than 15 percent. The biggest surge was in capital gains from stock sales. Capital gains realizations tripled between 1990 and 1998, to $60 billion.

On its face, Williams's discovery seemed like a positive outgrowth of the nascent dot-com boom. Kicked off by Yahoo's IPO in 1996, and fueled by stock market speculation in a slew of new Internet companies, the dot-com boom created instapreneurs and sudden wealth on a scale that the country hadn't seen since the railroad boom of the nineteenth century. California was hosting a new gold rush, and the fact that some of the gold dust was raining down on government seemed to confirm the state's ideal of shared prosperity.

Yet it wasn't truly shared. And for Williams, the emergence of these "two Californias" had more troubling implications. He had done enough research on tech stocks and financial markets to know that the forces behind the income boom—momentum investing, speculation, paying huge multiples for "eyeballs"—could quickly unwind. California's economy was becoming less reliant on its traditional pillars of aerospace, agriculture, real estate, and consumer sales, and increasingly reliant on stock market wealth that could vaporize overnight. An economy once built on real things was now built on paper.

In turn, California's tax revenues were also more volatile, balanced on a tiny sliver of the population. By 1998, the top 1 percent of earners in California were making 20 percent of the income, up from 14 percent in 1993, and paying 41 percent of the state's personal income taxes—more than the entire bottom 80 percent. While the rich taxpayers of California were small in number, their tax revenues rapidly eclipsed the money from the rest of the economy.

Williams had stumbled onto a problem that could be far more severe than any real estate bust or defense-spending slump. If most of the state's income-tax revenues were coming from the wealthy, and most of their wealth was coming from fickle stock markets, then California's revenues could crash with any sudden moves in the stock market.

"It seemed like we created a revenue cliff," he said.

When and how California's government would fall off that cliff remained unclear. It all depended on the stock market. So in 1998 and 1999, Brad Williams decided that the entire business of forecasting California's economy and tax revenues had to change.

To keep doing his job, he needed to reinvent himself. Looking at the wages and salaries for the whole state no longer had as much value. What he really needed to understand was the economy of the paper millionaires in Silicon Valley. He needed to become a plutologist.

So he began poring over SEC filings for Yahoo, Apple, and other California tech giants to better understand the stock holdings and stock sales patterns for the top executives. He followed the companies' earnings releases and studied models on stock option pricing and volatility.

Since among the rich, stock sales are often discretionary and driven in part by psychology—they might buy on optimism and sell on pessimism, rather than on financial need—Williams tried to better understand the mind-set of the wealthy. He met with financial advisors to the rich, asking them about their clients' investment plans and planned stock sales.

Yet the advisor meetings, like many of his new research tools, proved to be less reliable than his old methods of forecasting.

"The advisors were usually wrong," Williams said. "They would tell me, 'Oh, these guys are going to be selling their stock,' and then they'd hold on to it. It was very difficult to figure out where these stocks were going or what the wealthy were planning to do with their holdings."

Williams quickly realized that predicting the stock sales of the rich was largely futile. To accurately forecast the financial future of the rich, he realized, he had to predict the stock market. And that, he noted, "is impossible, as we all know."

He also realized that the California state government wasn't responding to his warnings of an impending bust and its consequences. In 2000, he prepared a report for the government with the innocuous title "California's Changing Income Distribution." Its message was more dire: most of the state's income growth—and by extension its tax revenues—was coming from a small group of highfliers with the state's most unstable incomes.

"The shifting distribution has helped state revenues to surge in the past five years, made revenues more volatile and raised the share of taxes paid by higher-income Californians," the report said.

He added that capital gains "can fluctuate substantially from one year to the next" and that state tax collections were suddenly "subject to more volatility than in the past." The report also warned of the political and social implications of "concentrations of economic and political power," in which "certain individuals can become mired at the low end of the distribution with no easy way of moving up."

Williams wasn't the only one noticing the state's growing dependence on the wealthy, of course. Economists and governors had for years lamented the state's dependence on its top earners. Yet whenever the volatility issue was raised by the governor or legislatures, it became a political football. Republicans argued that the surest way to reduce a looming budget crash and volatility in state revenues was to lower taxes on the highest earners. Democrats called the volatility issue a red herring, saying the real issue was widening income inequality, which was creating a surge in incomes for the elite and widespread poverty and stagnation for the rest of the state. They preferred to spend the money from the rich while they had it rather than worrying about its end.

"In California government, it seems to be about getting as much as can, when you can and hope that you can keep it," says Roger Niello, a financial accountant and a Republican former state assemblyman. "People would rather get money now and have it taken away later than not getting it at all."

Williams wasn't interested in the political crusade. He was fiercely nonpartisan and more worried about the economic fallout from a crash. In 2001, his worst fears came true. When the dot-com bubble burst and markets froze after the September 11 terrorist attacks, stocks began a long slide that wiped out $4.7 trillion in wealth from U.S. markets.

California found itself in the midst of a trickle-down recession. The dot-com bust and ensuing recession created a mirror image of the boom, with the wealthy leading the crash and dragging tax revenues down with them. The state's revenue from capital gains plummeted 66 percent, from $17 billion to $6 billion, while personal income taxes fell 32 percent, largely because of declines at the top. By 2002, California had a budget shortfall of more than $20 billion.

Williams didn't predict the recession. In fact, his budget statement from 2000 was fairly optimistic, calling for "continued growth." Yet he had identified the risks of high-beta wealth and tried to bring them to the attention of the state's politicians. And few very people took notice.

"I wouldn't say they ignored me," Williams says. "I think they listened, and some of them understood the message. But I just don't think it was a priority."

The multibillion-dollar deficit lingered for years. Yet the lessons of the dot-com bust and of Williams's analysis were quickly forgotten in the state capital. By 2005, California was enjoying another surge in spending fueled by the incomes of the wealthy. In 2004, state revenue collectors received a $200 million check from a single Google executive selling stock, according to state officials. (The check was too big for the state's collection system, so they asked the filer to break it down into smaller checks).

Williams once again began to sound the alarms. In 2005, he released a report stating that the state's tax revenues could vary by as much as $12 billion in a single year, and that such swings were "more likely than not." He wrote that the state tax system had become even more vulnerable after the dot-com bust and that stocks were poised for more radical swings.

"We believe that significant revenue volatility will continue to be a major characteristic of California's tax system, absent major policy changes to the tax system's structure," he wrote.

This time he offered potential fixes, which fell into two broad categories: fixing the tax structure to make it less volatile, or putting in place better planning tools to manage the volatility.

The way California's government worked at the time was that the state would treat each year's windfall from the rich as a recurring income stream, allocating the money to long-term programs in education, health care, pensions or other areas. When the revenues from the rich dried up, the spending continued, leading to multibillion-dollar budget shortfalls.

Williams's first approach involved broadening the tax base. This could be done by lowering the tax rate on capital gains, making the tax code less progressive, increasing other kinds of taxes (such as the sales tax) to reduce the role of income taxes, or using income averaging, which would spread out tax payments more evenly out over multiple years.

For the second approach, Williams suggested that the state set aside more money during booms for a rainy-day fund. The state had long had such a fund, but it was never large enough to offset recessions. He also recommended that the state spend the biggest windfalls on onetime projects such as roads, bridges, or paying down debt, so the state would avoid long-term commitments it couldn't meet.

"The message was, 'Hey, we've got a real problem here in California, and if we want to try to solve it, here are some choices,'" he said. "I wasn't telling them what to do. But at least they had some choices."

The state legislators, however, weren't interested. Democratic leaders in the legislature were loath to lower taxes on the wealthy, especially with the middle class eroding and the rich getting

richer and earning more and more of the income growth. Republicans often wanted to lower taxes or return any excess money to
the taxpayers.

As the money rolled in throughout the 2000s—from tech
companies, the real estate boom, and finance—it was commit-
ted to long-term government programs. The state's dependence
on the paper millionaires continued to grow. By 2007, the top 1
percent of California's taxpayers were back to earning 25 percent
of all income and paying 48 percent of the state's income taxes.

By 2007, Williams was growing increasingly frustrated with
state government.

"I was like a broken record," he said. "You can only keep saying the same thing so many times before you just get tired of it."

He was also becoming disenchanted with the whole notion
of forecasting the state economy and revenues. In the 1980s and
early 1990s, he'd been able to rely on the beautiful certainty of
numbers: state wage data, employment revisions, average salary
increases. But being a plutologist meant the impossible task of
predicting the stock market and the minds of millionaires.

In 2007, he decided to retire. Two years later, the real estate
bust and financial crisis wiped out half the value of the stock
market, and the incomes of the rich fell by three times as much
as those of the rest of the country. California suffered a tax crash
that was even worse than the dot-com bust. By 2011, the state was
racing to cut costs to fill a $26 billion budget hole.

On a sunny spring day in 2011, Williams is walking through
the wood-paneled halls of the state capitol. He looks relaxed and
cheery in a blue blazer and open collar. Yet the mood in the capitol is grim. A crowd of protestors has gathered in a hallway to protest cuts to state-supported business districts. They wear buttons
and hats that say "Save Jobs." There are protests almost every day

from similar groups, battling cuts in everything from health care and education to pensions.

Williams now works for a consulting firm that advises companies or institutions on the state budget process. Business is brisk, he says, since so many people and institutions have a stake in the cuts.

"It's very sad what's happening," Williams says as he winds his way through the crowds. "The sad thing is that even with all these cuts, the state hasn't really solved the real problem, which is the volatility."

As we exit the building and step out into the morning sunshine, I ask him if he feels any satisfaction in having predicted the problems stemming from California's wealth addiction.

"Maybe I should," he said. "But with this issue, there was no real pleasure in being right."

HIGH-BETA GOVERNMENT

Just as they've taken over the consumer economy with their outsize incomes, spending, and wealth, America's millionaires are also becoming the dominant funders of the federal and state governments.

The top 1 percent of Americans now earn 20 percent of the nation's income and pay more than 38 percent of its federal income taxes. For many state governments, their share is even higher. In New Jersey, the top 1 percent of earners paid 40 percent of incomes taxes in 2008. In New York, the top 1 percent pay about 42 percent, with Wall Street and the financial services business accounting for more than 20 percent of all state wages. In Connecticut, residents making more than $1 million a year (near the top half of the top 1 percent) accounted for more than a quarter of the state's income and income taxes.

Part of the increase is due to higher tax rates on the wealthy over the past decade. New York, California, Maryland, New Jersey, and other states have raised the top tax rates or created special "millionaire" taxes to boost revenue.

The bulk of the increase, however, is driven by the growing share of national income going to the top 1 percent. The top 1 percent of earners in the United States accounted for 20 percent of income in 2008, more than double their share in the "magic year" of 1982. In California, the top 1 percent accounted for a quarter of all state income, up from 14 percent in 1993. Even in states with flat taxes, where everyone pays the same income tax rate regardless of income, the wealthy now pay a higher share of taxes. Illinois has long had a 3 percent income tax rate regardless of income. Yet taxpayers making more than $500,000 now pay 30 percent of all income taxes, up from an inflation-adjusted 18 percent in 1995.

If America has become a land of representation without taxation, with the bottom 40 percent paying little or no federal income taxes, it's largely because so many Americans are now underrepresented in the country's income pyramid. More and more of the government's finances now rest on the very top of that pyramid, creating frequent swings and falls. In New York, the top 1 percent of taxpayers contribute more to the state's year-to-year tax volatility than all the other taxpayers combined. In a report downgrading New Jersey's credit rating in 2011, Standard and Poor's stated that New Jersey's wealth "translates into a high ability to pay taxes but might also contribute to potential revenue volatility."

The problems are most noticeable at the state level, since the states are required to balance their budgets. State budget problems after the 2008 recession sparked a wave of public protest in Wisconsin, New Jersey, New York, and California, as well as mass layoffs of teachers, firefighters, police, and other public servants. Republicans blame runaway spending, public employee pensions, and unions. Democrats blame excessive tax cuts for the rich. Yet as you can see from the table below, the trouble with state budgets is a drop in revenue, not of a sudden rise in spending. And in many states, that drop was caused by the falling incomes of the rich.

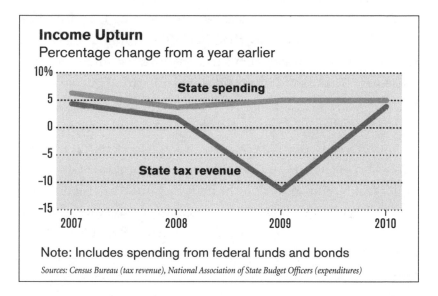

Income Upturn
Percentage change from a year earlier

Note: Includes spending from federal funds and bonds

Sources: Census Bureau (tax revenue), National Association of State Budget Officers (expenditures)

Tax experts say the problems of high-beta government are likely to spread to Washington as the growing income gap widens and wealth becomes more unstable.

"These revenues have a narcotic effect on legislatures," said Greg Torres, president of MassINC, a nonpartisan think tank that's researched tax revenues from the wealthy. "They become numb to the trend and think the revenue picture is improving, but they don't realize the money is ephemeral."

The question is, how can states and governments around the world kick their high-beta wealth habit without making inequality even worse?

Roger Niello knows both sides of the high-beta government problem. His family owns Niello Auto Group, one of the largest car dealership groups around Sacramento, which sells luxury brands such as Porsche, Maserati, Land Rover, and Jaguar. During the good times, the dealerships throw off mountains of cash, putting Niello comfortably among the top 1 percent of taxpayers in the state, he says.

Yet in 2009, luxury car sales ground to a halt, and Niello's family income fell by more than half. "I'm still fine financially, you don't need to worry about me," he jokes, sitting in a small office near Sacramento in a plaid shirt and jeans. "But we took a big hit."

His knowledge of things rich has also led him to focus on the dangers of California's tax code when he was in the state assembly between 2004 and 2010 (he left because of the state's term limit of six years). While on the budget committee, Niello studied Brad Williams's research and became an advocate of trying to reduce income-tax volatility. As a moderate Republican, however, he frustrated both die-hard conservatives and left-leaning Democrats.

Niello helped push a ballot initiative that would have helped create a stronger rainy-day fund for California. The initiative would have increased the mandatory deposits into the fund, raised its maximum limit, and restricted how the fund could be spent. It also allowed half the payments into the fund to be used for one-time projects or debt payments. Under the plan, the state would create a baseline growth target, based on long-term historical trends, and use all revenues above that trend line for the fund.

The initiative, however, died at the ballot box. Democrats opposed putting a cap on spending, while Republicans opposed an extension of a tax hike that was attached to the measure.

"It was a rare moment when both the extreme right and extreme left came together to oppose something," one state senator told me.

A special tax commission set up by former governor Arnold Schwarzenegger to overhaul the tax system also tried to tackle the volatility problem. "The boom-and-bust economic cycles the current tax system depends on have turned our state budgeting system into an unpredictable roller-coaster ride that brings windfalls one year and deficits the next," Schwarzenegger said.

The commission recommended lowering tax rates for everyone, eliminating the corporate tax and sales tax, creating a new tax on business receipts, and building a stronger rainy-day fund. The recommendations were rejected by many in the legislature, especially by Democrats. Some even lampooned the fears over volatility and the commission's recommendations. California state senator Noreen Evans wrote a blog post in 2009 titled "The Volatility Monster—Be Afraid, Be Very Afraid."

> The Commission and governor suggest that the source of our budget woes is a sinister monster called—(cue scary music)— "revenue volatility." As their story goes, if we slay the revenue volatility monster all our budget problems will disappear. So we have no choice but to give very rich people jaw-dropping tax cuts.
>
> Here is the real volatility problem. Very rich people pay a lot of income taxes when they make lots of money in good economic years. Their income taxes go down in recessions because they earn less money. Equity markets, stock options, bonuses, and capital gains depend upon the health of the economy, and with the economy, are volatile. As a result of accumulation of income

in a few hands, the state collects more in income taxes because our personal income tax is progressive.

The true response to solving the volatility problem is to make sure Californians are fully employed and decently paid. The Commission proposes reducing PIT (personal income tax) revenues under the fig leaf of stabilizing revenues. Using this logic, if California just stopped collecting taxes, the problem of volatility would be solved forever.

What may sound like yet another tired debate between the tax-the-rich left and anti-tax right may, however, be more of a side effect of more recent changes in wealth. Ajay Kapur, the plutonomy strategist, said the plutonomy creates an inherent imbalance in government, with a small group of rich plutonomists funding most of the government, while a great mass of non-plutonomists vanish in the income distribution and tax base.

The masses at the bottom require increased funding for entitlements and social programs. But those at the top, who are increasingly paying for those programs, will exert an outsize influence on politicians through their money and will lobby for lower tax rates. The result is that governments will have more booms and busts and permanent deficits, Kapur says.

"It's fascinating when you think about it, because on the one hand you have this large fraction of the population that doesn't pay any federal income tax but has all these demands for goodies," he said. "Then you have the plutonomists, who will protect their turf and taxes so the taxes they pay will never be enough to meet everyone else's demand. The conclusion is that budget deficits are biased toward getting bigger and bigger. Either you've got to cut down the demands of the population, which is very tough in a democracy. Or you have to raise revenues to pay for it. That's not happening either. This problem and the problem of volatility appear to be a manifestation of the plutonomy and democracy."

If government dependence on the rich is permanent and permanently unstable, is there anything governments can do?

The best hope, it seems, are people such as Brad Williams. A similar perspective comes from New York State's current budget director, Robert Megna, who has been fixated on taxes from the rich for more than a decade, after he realized that Wall Streeters were paying more and more of the state's taxes. Yet rather than trying to change the tax code or reduce taxes on bankers, Megna concentrated on using forecasts as a better planning tool.

He has a team of economists, for instance, that study pay on Wall Street to predict their pay. They look at quarterly earnings reports for Goldman Sachs, Morgan Stanley, JPMorgan Chase, and others and study how much the banks are setting aside each quarter for pay so that state forecasters aren't caught by surprise at the end of the year. "There's no getting around the fact that we are now very dependent on a relatively small slice of taxpayers, and that slice moves up and down a lot given economic conditions," he says.

Megna's most effective strategy is managing politics by managing economic expectations. When Wall Street has a blowout year and income tax revenues are up, say by 10 percent, Megna predicts the next year at about 5 percent. The state could still wind up with what Brad Williams called a "revenue cliff." But the cliff will be half the size. "What you really have to do is discipline yourself and the process to say, 'Hey, based on historical averages, we're not going to have another year like last one.' The key is to be conservative in the estimates."

Of course, boom periods usually drag on longer than expected, so eventually "you could grow at 10 percent for two or three years and people say we're too conservative."

In the end, however, Megna admits he couldn't hedge against the recessions of 2001 or 2009, or predict that a hedge fund manager who made $1 billion one year and paid more than $100 million in state taxes may pay nothing the next year. "Just because you can understand the volatility doesn't mean you can predict it," he says. While being miserly with the economic forecasts can help, ultimately the states and Washington will just have to start learning to live with the extreme ups and downs that come from relying on the rich.

"It's a curse and a blessing," Megna says. "Look, we're glad to have wealthy individuals who pay a significant fraction of our revenues, and we want to encourage those people to stay in New York and remain prosperous. It's a good thing to have [these wealthy taxpayers]," Megna said. "But you have to recognize that because you have them, you also have this extreme volatility. This is a new phenomenon for us, but sooner or later, everyone's going to have to deal with it."

PART IV

---●---

Solving for Beta

9

THE LOW-BETA RICH

In the post-1982 world, the surest way to make (and lose) a fast fortune was to borrow and speculate. Building sustainable businesses or making real products that improve our world may sound noble. But why bother when you can borrow at 2 percent, buy an asset, and flip it for a quick profit? Why settle for the trickle of an income stream when you can be awash in cash from a liquidity event?

Not all of the rich fell for the allures of high-beta wealth. While they are less visible than the flamboyant strivers such as the Blixseths and Siegels, the low-beta rich offer us lessons in how to build wealth today while avoiding the risks inherent in a post-1982 world. They are allergic to debt. They never buy anything unless they can pay cash. They try to avoid relying on a single stock or a single source of income to fund their lifestyle and retirement. They keep their spending modest. And some low-beta entrepreneurs keep their salaries to a minimum, preferring to live off their liquidity events.

David Gilmour, the multimillionaire founder of Fiji Water, Zinio, and nine other companies, says he hasn't taken a salary since the 1960s. He lives off the winnings of selling the companies he starts.

"I never take a salary, and never had a company car," he told me. "It's a waste. For me, it's about the best way to create long-term value, for me and my people."

His philosophy is similar to that of Frank Kavanaugh, another entrepreneur who could serve as a model for the low-beta rich.

LONELY AT THE TOP

Frank Kavanaugh gets nervous when times are good.

Maybe it's because of the hard knocks he took as a kid, dropping out of high school at seventeen and getting kicked out of his house. Maybe it's because he watched his dad—a highly respected California psychiatrist—get divorced three times and fall into a deep depression because of his debts.

Frank says it's because, like most rich people, "I'm just insecure."

Whatever the reason, by 2007, Frank Kavanaugh—a forty-seven-year-old tech entrepreneur, private equity chief, and former CEO—had no debts and more $100 million to invest. And he was worried.

Everyone around him seemed wildly optimistic about the economy and wealth. Living on the prosperous shores of Laguna Beach, in the heart of California's real estate boom, Frank had countless friends who were getting hugely rich using borrowed money. They were buying homes and buildings, flipping them for profits, and borrowing even more to do it all over again.

With their easy winnings, they bought new vacation homes, sports cars, boats, and planes. It was no accident that the nation's largest Lamborghini dealership was in Orange County, California.

Meanwhile, Frank was living in a modest home with his family of five, with no mortgage, no debt, and a five-year-old SUV. Usually dressed in cargo shorts and a T-shirt, with a bright smile and close-cut dark hair, Frank has the look of an amiable corporate executive from the Sun Belt. He is prone to wisecracks and witty one-liners. But his genial façade hides a deep skepticism and an aversion to following crowds.

Frank preferred to stay home and read (mostly science fiction) rather than socialize. He tried joining a wealth club called Tiger 21, which brings together millionaires to give each other financial advice and personal support. But none of them wanted to hang around Frank.

"He wasn't too popular," laughs his wife, Susan. "They would all say, 'If you want to jump off a cliff, go talk to Frank.'"

Frank had a name for the Tiger 21 crowd and most of the newly rich in Southern California. He called them the "bubble people." He didn't dislike them, blame them, or think he was smarter. He just thought they were wrong. "The bubble people are not bad people. They were all extremely intelligent and successful. They were acting rationally in the system in which they lived."

There were times—many times, in fact—when Frank envied the bubble people. They made it look so easy. And they were happy. While Frank went around talking about the next financial apocalypse and scrolling through doom-and-gloom blogs on the Web, the bubble people were hosting parties at their newly built mansions and talking about their newest cars, boats, and planes.

"I envied these people, I really did," he says.

Susan asks, "You did?"

"Sure. I wondered for a while whether I was a complete idiot for not doing what they were doing."

Yet deep down, Frank couldn't shake his fear throughout the mid-2000s that things were about to go horribly wrong. His anxiety had its roots in research he had been doing for over a decade on investing, after he sold his second company and had tens of millions of dollars to invest.

He had read investor Harry Dent's books, including *The Next Great Bubble Boom*. Dent helped to popularize the "spending wave" theory, which argued that the baby boomers would start spending and investing less as they entered retirement and started downsizing their lives. He argued that the peak for their spending would be between 2007 and 2009. After that, their lower spending and investment would lead to a weaker economy and falling stock markets.

Frank also read a stack of books on value investing, starting with the classic *Security Analysis* by market legends Benjamin Graham and David D. Dodd. He especially liked Chapter 7, which discussed the difference between speculation and investing based on underlying values.

"A lot of what I saw looked more like speculation than investing," he notes.

Along with books about the Great Depression, Frank had also started to read bearish blogs by investment gurus such as Michael Shedlock and economist Nouriel Roubini.

By 2007 and 2008, when the debt markets started to falter and housing sales began to slow, Frank felt that the world was poised for a deep financial crisis. So much of the previous decade of growth and wealth creation had been fueled by debt, excess liquidity, and rising asset prices. Now that all three were coming under pressure, Frank believed that the United States was headed for its day of reckoning.

He didn't hope to make a fortune from the fall. By his own admission, Frank is not a professional investor, or even a sophisticated one. He didn't have a specific trade idea to express his theory of impending disaster.

"I wasn't like Michael Burry or John Paulson," he said, two hedge fund managers who made billions from shorting the housing market in 2008 and 2009. "I didn't know about shorting subprime mortgages or CDOs or any of that stuff."

Frank is an engineer and tech geek at heart. His obsession is starting companies, creating jobs, and reinventing industries, from computer software to military vehicles. His talent is in finding a new way to approach a business.

"I see a company or product and I'm always asking myself, 'How could that be done differently or better?'" Frank says.

He also has a knack for peering into the future. Frank calls it "seeing around corners." But a friend and business colleagues say he has a sixth sense for coming economic trends. What Frank saw in 2008 was the end of the bubble economy and a potential collapse of the U.S. banking system and currency. At the time he was between businesses. He had just left his biggest company—an armored vehicle manufacturer—and had yet to start the next one. So his only goal as an investor headed into the storm was to find a safe place for his cash.

He avoided stocks, hedge funds, real estate, private equity, and all the other fashionable investments. He put his money into U.S. Treasuries, bonds, and cash. He also put on his "apocalypse trade"—opening up a Swiss bank account (fully registered and compliant with U.S. banking laws) and filling it with Swiss francs, Singapore dollars, and euros.

Frank always doubts himself. So he put about 15 percent of his fortune with a highly respected hedge fund manager. He also handed over a small chunk to Credit Suisse to invest.

By 2010, his Treasuries and Swiss bank accounts had maintained their value. The hedge fund investment had plunged by 60 percent. Credit Suisse lost his entire investment in a month.

Thanks to his own trades and pessimism, Frank Kavanaugh emerged from the Great Recession with total losses of about 10 percent or less.

"I don't want to come off as this brilliant investment guy," Frank says, sitting on the sofa of his home overlooking the Pacific. "I had brain damage like everyone else. Those losses still drive me crazy. And I've had my ass handed to me plenty of times in the past by buying some stupid stock. But I think this time around I just got lucky. Really, I got lucky."

Frank, who shies away from media attention unless it's on his companies, insists it's wrong to hold him out as an example of wealth wisdom during the crisis. "The only reason I didn't blow up is because I just happened not to be in the real estate business. If I had been in real estate, I would have taken the same hit everyone else did. It's just by accident, really, that I am where I am."

Accident and luck may have played roles. But Frank Kavanaugh's success during the financial crisis, and his ability to accumulate more than $100 million in wealth without becoming a high beta, has deeper roots. It stems from his wayward and unconventional childhood, his family money history, his introverted nature, and the strong partnership and shared frugality with his wife.

When he was seventeen, Frank barged into his house and announced to his stepmom he was quitting school. He was in his senior year of high school in the affluent beach town of La Jolla, California, and after he had decided not to attend a class he hated, the school principal told him he had to go to summer school. Frank told the principal: "I'm not going to summer school. I quit."

When he got home, he gave his parents the same proclamation. His stepmother, who had endured years of Frank's truancy and lack of motivation, gave him a simple response.

"She told me, 'If you're not going to school, you're not going to live here anymore,'" Frank recalls. "And she was serious. She helped me find an apartment. She gave me three cooking pans and a mattress and wished me luck. She was very sweet about it, but tough. Looking back on it, it was very lovingly done."

Yet after growing up in the privileged home of a well-known psychiatrist father and a supportive stepmom, Frank was on his own. He had no job, no real skills, and no real friends.

"You can ask what kind of psychological or intellectual stuff was behind all this, but the answer is pretty simple," Frank says. "I was a stupid seventeen-year-old."

He also had no real calling or driving passions. School didn't really interest him. Neither did sports, science, or anything, really, except for girls and cars. He always did the minimum amount required. To get his driver's license in his junior year, for example, his dad told him he needed to get a B-minus average.

"So that's exactly what I got, a got a B-minus," Frank says.

After getting kicked out of his house, he drifted from job to job. He worked as a busboy, carpenter, and bartender. He partied and drank a lot. When I asked him about role models or mentors at that time in his life, he said, "Jose Cuervo?"

On the morning he turned twenty-one, Frank woke up and decided his life needed to change. The drinking, the manual labor, and the low pay had turned him into a listless wanderer. Other friends the same age were graduating from college with degrees and were getting high-paying office jobs. So on his twenty-first birthday, he enrolled in a junior college. He quickly earned an economics degree, then transferred to the University of California at Irvine and got a degree in computer science.

Computers were not an obvious choice for Frank. He wasn't a childhood programming prodigy like Bill Gates or other successful tech stars. Frank liked technology. But he had never spent much time with computers growing up in the 1980s.

"I chose computer science for two reasons," Frank says. "Because I thought it would pay well and it was easy."

In his senior year, he became fascinated by artificial intelligence and dreamed about working on advanced robotics. But after graduating, he decided to take a more practical job as a systems engineer at Hewlett-Packard and later at Microsoft.

At Microsoft, Frank met his wife, Susan, a rising systems engineer who had also grown up in Southern California. Petite, fit, and fiercely intelligent, Susan had gotten two computer degrees from Loyola Marymount University before landing high-ranking jobs at IBM and Microsoft. She had always followed the twin virtues of thrift and hard work: as one of six children of a frugal aerospace engineer, she had worked her way through college and high school serving burgers at McDonald's and working behind the counter at a rental car company.

As Frank puts it: "She's the family overachiever."

In 1988, Frank decided to strike out on his own and start a business. At Microsoft, he spotted a need for a company that could train IT professionals on how to use Microsoft applications. He formed QuickStart Intelligence. The firm quickly grew to become one of the leading Microsoft training companies.

In 1992, Frank sold his stake in QuickStart to a venture capital firm for $1.8 million. For most couples, the payday would have marked the start of the good life. They were, at thirty-four, suddenly millionaires.

"It felt like more money than we would ever need," Frank says. The typical path would have been to "go out and be wealthy and exchange pictures of dead presidents and suddenly expect my life would get better."

But Frank and Susan were smarter than that. Both of them had always been careful with money, based on their family histories. At one point, Frank's dad wound up in the hospital with severe depression because of his finances.

"I said to myself that I would never let that happen to me," he says.

Frank also had a strange set of personality quirks that helped him avoid getting caught up in bubbles. He is a loner. "I've always been an introvert. I have no friends," he says, only partially kidding. His tendency to pelt people with questions, even in social situations, often leaves him relying on his wife for invitations. "After people meet us, they say, 'Oh, we loved Susan. . . . ' "

He also tends to see the glass as half empty.

"I'm a pessimist about things that I can't control directly," he says. "If I'm not involved, I'm less confident in the outcomes."

It's not that Frank thinks he's superior. Quite the opposite. By his own admission, he has what might be considered an inferiority complex. One of his theories about rich people is that they're motivated in large part by insecurities tracing back to their childhood, parents, or early adulthood. At UC Irvine, when he was among the oldest but least educated in his class, he became used to life as "the dumbest guy in the room."

"Even today, when I walk into a meeting or conversation, I assume I'm the dumbest one in the room." This perspective, he says, has helped him enormously.

"Insecurity is a great driver," he says. "I have friends who are normal, well-balanced people and they do fine, but people with insecurities seem to be willing to work a little bit harder. It's that extra push."

Susan, for her part, is far more well adjusted. But she is careful about money, having learned to be a disciplined saver and planner from her father, who would delight in finding pennies on the floor and always drove old cars.

"He was so frugal, and a terrific investor," she says. "We never did anything flashy growing up. It was all about work and saving."

Before they got married, Frank and Susan sat down and came up with a detailed financial plan for the rest of their lives, breaking out their targeted spending, incomes, and savings rates. It was all geared toward achieving a specific target: a retirement fund of $8 million.

To meet their goal, they lived in a modest home with their three children. They avoided all debts, including mortgages. And they drove a practical Toyota.

Frank also had an unusual approach to salaries. Large salaries, he believes, are what spoil people and lead them to outsize lifestyles. So at QuickStart, Frank paid himself only $20,000 a year. Most of his compensation came in the form of stock, which would be cashed in if and when the company was sold.

The approach not only helped him keep the family expenses low but also made him more motivated to build the value of the company. His incentives were now long-term rather than short-term. His wealth came from keeping cash in the company, not from taking it out.

"Large salaries are what kills you," he said. "It's the most detrimental thing you can have. Your lifestyle just grows to fill the salary, so pretty soon you need $250,000 just to get out of bed in the morning."

To Frank, a large salary lulls people into thinking that the money will never stop, that they can borrow and spend beyond their current means because they'll make even more next year. They view their wealth as a never-ending stream, rather than the momentary shower. Sure, they may be overextended on the boat and the plane and the two homes,. But it's nothing a few years of high salaries can't fix. Frank is different. He spends only what he has now, and invests for the longer term. In 1993, he helped start a second company, called NewGen Systems, a digital-imaging company. When it was sold five years later, Frank made $5 million. At NewGen, he also took a minimal salary.

After the sale, the Kavanaughs were well past their $8 million. The proceeds from the two companies, along with their savings, investment returns, and Microsoft stock, put them well into the eight figures. Now that they had all the money they thought they'd dreamed of, Frank started dabbling in conspicuous consumption—usually with comical results.

In 1994, shortly after the NewGen sale, Frank and Susan decided to take the family to Ireland. Family travel and education were the two areas where they agreed that spending large amounts of money was actually worth it. Yet when they arrived at the airport, they found themselves stuck on an endless line for check-in on economy class. They were about to miss their flight. Frank went up to the first-class counter—which had no line—and bought first-class tickets for the entire family. They cost $12,000.

"When I was standing on that line, I just thought, 'Hey, we're rich, we don't have to stand on this line,'" Frank says.

They boarded the flight and had a memorable trip. But Frank started regretting the expense almost immediately.

"We had just bought a new Toyota Camry for $21,460," Frank says. "And I remember as soon as I bought the airline tickets, I realized they cost half as much as the Camry. I kept thinking, 'Half a Camry, for one flight!'"

Adds Susan, "I told him not to do it. I thought it was terrible."

To this day, Frank still refers to the vacation as the "half a Camry" trip.

He also had an awkward flirtation with private jets. When he was younger, Frank promised himself that if he ever made it into the eight figures with wealth, he would fly on private jets. After the NewGen sale, Frank bought a jet card that gave him twenty-five hours of private-jet flight time. Most families would burn through twenty-five hours over Christmas and Easter. It took the Kavanaughs over two years to use the hours because they felt so guilty about the cost. They wound up using most of the flights to visit their son in boarding school, rather than jetting off to Cabo or Aspen for the weekends.

"As soon as you buy it, the rational part of you kicks in and you realize, 'This is so stupid,'" Frank says. "It felt too extravagant."

For his fortieth birthday, Frank bought a Porsche. It was used and he got a great deal. But after six weeks, he returned it and settled back into his old Lexus 400 LS sedan.

"I just didn't like the Porsche," he said. "It wasn't my thing."

To be sure, the Kavanaughs live well. They are not the millionaires next door, living in a blue-collar town, driving old Ford Fiestas, and reheating meat loaf for dinner. Their house is a 6,000-square-foot Mediterranean overlooking the Pacific in Dana Point, California—an ultra-wealthy enclave with an average house price of $4 million.

They take exotic vacations to Africa, Asia, and the Caribbean. The day I visited them, they were about to head to the Galapagos Islands. They belong to a destination club in which members pay tens of thousands of dollars to stay in a collection of private mansions or apartments around the world.

The Kavanaughs recently bought their first vacation home—a small house on a quiet island near Seattle. The home has its own airplane hangar, which Frank figured would be a good investment in the long run.

"Our focus has always been to use money to create opportuni-

ties for our kids, and on things that bring our family closer together. If we can't do that, what's the point of all the money? It's
just money—it doesn't have anything magical."

In 2008, Frank cashed out of his biggest company yet—Force
Protection, the first U.S. manufacturer of armored vehicles that
supplied mine-resistant trucks to the military. Frank had been
the CEO and largest shareholder. When he discovered the company in 2001, it was a struggling manufacturer of speedboats.
He invested $25,000 and shifted its focus from boats to armored
vehicles. By the time he left the company, Force Protection had
more than $1 billion in defense contracts, and Frank's $25,000
stake had grown to more than $60 million.

The stress of running Force Protection took its toll. It was
his first public company, so there was the constant pressure of
quarterly earnings and shareholders. Worse yet was the anxiety of
being responsible for the lives of U.S. soldiers in Iraq. Force Protection vehicles performed well—no Marine had ever died in one
as the result of an improvised explosive device.

"But I'd wake up every night worrying about it," Frank says.

So after leaving the company, he decided to slow down. He
founded a group called Prosperitas, which gathered millionaires,
entrepreneurs, and great thinkers together for regular meetings at
the UC Irvine campus. He caught up on his sleep. He spent more
time with his kids.

His semi-retirement lasted for all of a year.

"To me, the excitement comes from finding a new way to do
something, and to create jobs. That's what excites me."

So in 2010, he founded his next venture, an insurance company. Susan is a little puzzled, since insurance "sounds kind of
boring for Frank." But Frank can talk passionately for a half hour
about the "broken business model" of the insurance industry and
his ideas to fix it.

"I'm sorry," he says after finishing his little speech. "Insurance gets me worked up these days."

What gets him even more worked up is the state of the wealthy. Life as a low-beta millionaire is one of perpetual frustration and disbelief. There is always someone else making more money with less work and discipline. Low betas take comfort in knowing that someday their time will come. They live and work under the assumption that someday America will once again reward people who create lasting companies and jobs.

For Frank and other low betas, the Great Recession was only a partial reckoning. Lots of reckless investors and real estate speculators lost their fortunes. But Wall Street and the entire industry of financial engineering and trading remained largely untouched. The low betas were never really vindicated the way they'd hoped.

"What's unfortunate is that we continue to reward people for not creating sustainable real value," he says. "Look at the banking system. It's reemerged, and even after what these people did, the compensation system remained in place, and they had to be paid bonuses to stay. I know a lot of very smart, very nice people at Goldman Sachs. But they don't really have expertise in a real business, and I'm not sure they're creating real lasting value."

Sitting on his couch overlooking the Pacific Ocean, Frank looks out at a crowd of surfers and the setting sun. He's the first to argue that he doesn't deserve his success. He says it's mostly luck, a result of showing up at the right place at the right time. But he hopes that sometime in the future, America's wealthy will have to earn and preserve wealth the hard way—by starting companies and filling a need.

"Maybe I'm being naive," he said. "But we need to reinvent the idea of wealth in this country."

EPILOGUE

The Future of High-Beta Wealth

By the fall of 2011, the risks and rewards of high-beta wealth were higher than ever. New bubbles are forming in tech stocks, gold, and other far-flung corners of the financial world. The 2011 initial public offering of LinkedIn, the social-media company, valued the company at more than $8 billion—despite its having no projected profits in 2011—setting in motion a new cycle of stock-based hyper-wealth that could rival or exceed the mid-2000s. LinkedIn's founder, Reid Hoffman, was worth more than $1.5 billion, a stunning rise for an angel investor who in 2004 labeled his status in Silicon Valley as "embarrassing," since he was a mere millionaire. Facebook, Groupon, Zynga, and other companies are quickly joining the IPO conga line, trailing behind them a new parade of paper billionaires.

Once again, finance is fueling the party and creating ever more mini booms and crashes. During one four-day period in the summer of 2011, the S&P 500 Index rose and fell more than 4 percent each day for four straight days. The river of money flowing into stocks and other investments is now more global than ever, gathering cash from Chinese savers, Middle East governments, Brazilian companies, and other tributaries. This fast-moving capital is likely to make bubbles and busts larger and more frequent than ever. Investors will charge in, herd-like, to the hottest investments and rush for the exits at the moment when reality sets in. Everyday materials like silver or cocoa are becoming financial trading instruments and sources of speculation, leading to huge price swings. Silver prices more than doubled over the course of a year, then plunged in 2011.

All this financial froth has encouraged the rich to return to their boom-time ways. While many of the rich who lost money have become far more cautious in their investing and spending (especially the aging baby boomers), the younger millionaires and billionaires are spending, borrowing, and betting just like they were in the mid-2000s. By the end of 2010, America's top-earning 5 percent accounted for 37 percent of consumer outlays. Those top 5 percenters also have the lowest savings rate of any income group in the country, saving just 1.4 percent of their income compared to more than 8 percent for the rest of Americans. The wealthy, who were once America's most savvy savers, are now the nation's biggest spendthrifts.

The next cycle of high-beta wealth has begun.

The financial crisis didn't end high-beta wealth. It may have even made it worse, both by encouraging reckless wealth and by increasing the trickle-down risks. What many are calling a freak "two-speed recovery"—with the rich benefiting from rebounding financial markets and the rest of America mired in unemployment and low housing prices—may prove to be a more permanent state for the economy, as the wealthy are best able to capitalize on overseas growth, technological change, and financial markets. Their share of the nation's income and wealth will likely continue to rise, with the top 1 percent accounting for 20 percent of the income and 34 percent of the wealth.

As the global investor Marc Faber told *Barron's* in the summer of 2011:

> The world has a dual economy. In the economy of the super-rich, Bentleys and Rolls-Royces and Ferraris and Porsches sit in front of fancy hotels . . . the people who own equities and commodities have done very well. At the same time, the economy of the workers and lower middle class is doing very badly. Wage increases don't match cost-of-living increases.

In this economy of Richistan and the rest, the rich will command a greater share of the U.S. and global economy. Luxury companies and businesses that serve the affluent will have the fastest growth and strongest profits. States that have the most millionaires will have the biggest surges in revenue in the coming years. We may even have another butler shortage.

Yet the growing dependence on the wealthy will lead to more instability, as we all ride the highs and lows of high-beta wealth. State and federal governments will be prone to California-style "revenue cliffs." The consumer economy will be mirroring the crazed patterns of stocks rather than the smooth lines of GDP and economic growth. Financial markets will become more wild with speculative money. Ken Cage, the repo man of the rich, will have a bright future filled with Gulfstreams and Sea Rays.

SOLVING BETA

It would be nice at this stage of the book to offer my grand solution. To say, "Here are the three easy ways to solve high-beta wealth," like Al Gore's helpful tip at the end of *An Inconvenient*

Truth to change to energy-efficient lightbulbs so we can reduce carbon emissions.

Yet there is no easy fix for high-beta wealth. To solve the problem of high-beta wealth requires solving two much bigger problems: the financialization of wealth and rising inequality. Governments show no sign of truly reining in financial markets or shrinking the amount of "hot money" racing around the world. And while Congress may tinker with new rules on regulating certain U.S. financial markets, the rise of finance is global and beyond the reach of any single government. Whatever new U.S. rules there might be will likely be misguided, ineffective, or both.

As for inequality, economists can't even agree on a cause, let alone a solution. Some argue that lower taxes on the rich have led to the growing wealth gap and the shrinking of the middle class. If we just raise their taxes, all would be well, they say. Others argue that the skills-based economy is the cause, and if we improved education and training, worker salaries would magically rise. Others say it's globalization, and that we just need a better industrial policy and trade barriers.

Whatever the real cause—more likely a combination of technology, globalization, and finance—inequality isn't likely to be "solved" by government anytime soon. The issues get reduced to oversimplified debates about taxing the rich or shrinking government or punishing Goldman Sachs—all of which may be politically satisfying and maybe even helpful, but far from a solution. They would be treating smaller symptoms of a much larger imbalance caused by the finance-fueled fortunes of the global rich driving most of our booms and busts.

So is there anything we can do to stop high-beta wealth? Is there any sign of hope or optimism in this new view of our economy? Happily, there is.

Even if we can't solve high-beta wealth, there are some things we can do to better manage the impacts. Following are five tips for governments, companies, and individuals for how to best survive (and occasionally prosper) in the age of high-beta wealth.

Follow the Money (in stocks)

Alan Greenspan, the former Federal Reserve chairman who is often blamed for the era of easy money, is now something of a Cassandra about inequality and the nation's finances. One big problem, he says, is that much of the economy depends on the spending of the wealthy. And much of that spending, he says, is determined by the daily whims of the stock market.

"One thing that we don't pay enough attention to in the economics profession is the fact that the stock market is not merely an indicator, it's a cause of economic activity," he told CNBC. "It's not paper profits, but the capital gains themselves have a very significant economic consequence . . . it is the higher-income brackets which do most of the spending." He added that "ordinarily we're saying that the stock market is driven by economic events; I think it's more in the reverse."

Stocks are highly unpredictable, of course. They move up and down each day for reasons that even the highest-paid investment professionals have trouble understanding. Yet in the age of high-beta wealth, most of the spending and taxpaying in America will be directed by the stock market. As Greenspan noted, stocks are no longer just measurements of growth and decline, but the main drivers of both. In an economy dominated by the rich, S&P is the new GDP.

What employees, businesses, and governments need to understand is that there is no such thing as "the American economy" anymore: there is the rich and the rest, with the rich increasingly determining our booms and busts. So to better predict where our nation's spending, taxes, and jobs may be headed, we need to watch the stock market and capital gains rather than broad measures like economic growth and wages. Following stocks, for instance, might have allowed states like California and New Jersey to better predict their swings in capital-gains revenues and avoid unnecessary budget cuts.

Take Money off the Table

As the economy becomes more manic, governments, companies, and individuals need to save more during booms so they can ride out the busts. They also need to plan for the worst-case scenarios. Managing wealth is now about managing risk.

This is a lesson already learned by the tech tycoons. Unlike the 1990s dot-com founders, who kept their entire fortunes tied up in company stock through the peaks and crashes, the chiefs of Facebook, LinkedIn, and the new generation of tech darlings are cashing out a portion of their stakes while times are good. Eric Leftkofsky, who helped found Groupon with a $1 million investment, has a stake potentially worth $4 billion, but he's already cashed out more than $300 million in private stock sales.

Governments should do the same. Whether or not taxes increase for the wealthy, tax revenues will come mostly from the volatile incomes of the highest earners. Governments can better plan for high-beta wealth by building in the potential for steep drops in their budget models. They can also create rainy-day funds (like the one created by Massachusetts) that will fund them through downturns.

"The dependence on the wealthy is both a blessing and a curse," Megna said. "The way to protect yourself is to be conservative with your estimates and expand the rainy-day funds."

Stop Acting Rich

Expecting the rich to change their culture or curb their excesses is probably a lost cause. The world of wealth is now defined by lottery-like liquidity events, constant borrowing, and a consumer-oriented society built on status goods, whether it's a seat at Davos or a seat on a G550. As wealth becomes more global and larger in scale, and luxury becomes more pervasive, the arms race of conspicuous consumption is likely to become even more competitive. As the low-beta Frank Kavanaugh said, "The rich will act according to the incentives of the system, and today's system of wealth rewards risk."

Yet the rest of us would do well to stop acting like the high betas, mimicking their borrowing and spending and manias. They can afford it (most of the time). We can't.

In his 2009 book *Stop Acting Rich . . . and Start Acting Like a Real Millionaire*, Thomas J. Stanley (coauthor of *The Millionaire Next Door*) argues that real millionaires owe their success to "integrity, discipline, social skills, a supportive spouse, leadership qualities, and having a love for one's vocation." For most of us, he says wealth is a "long-distance marathon" rather than a sprint, and "the only way you will become rich is to play extraordinary defense like those millionaires at the other end do the continuum: by living below your means, by planning, saving, and investing."

This may not make you super-rich, of course. But given the odds, most of us are better off playing financial defense.

Don't Be Fooled by All That Glitters

It's easier to look rich today than ever before. People can lease a Ferrari, rent a seat on a private jet, and live in mansions that are worth less than the mortgage. They may have huge paper wealth but little "real" cash wealth. Like that cardboard cutout of the couple in Aspen who were selling their mansion to pay the bills, today's rich often project the image of success but can be knocked down in the slightest of financial storms.

We've all read about the wealth-based reality shows on TV, where the diamond-draped "Real Housewives" parade their riches onscreen, while offscreen they're facing bankruptcy or foreclosure. They weren't really rich. They're TV rich.

As a culture, we need to take a more cautious approach to the wealthy. Just because someone looks rich doesn't mean they are. And since wealth is now less stable, today's rich may be tomorrow's debtors. Companies, governments, charities, and workers who rely on the wealthy need to do better due diligence on the foundations of wealth. Working for a millionaire who sold a business and is earning cash from investments is likely to be more stable than working for a time-share developer whose entire fortune is tied up in the company.

This sounds obvious. But it's a lesson that's widely overlooked. Consider the example of Birthright, a New York charity. Birthright was launched to provide Jewish adults a free trip to Israel to better understand their cultural and religious roots. In 2006, Sheldon Adelson, the billionaire gambling tycoon, pledged to give the charity $25 million a year. Birthright expanded its program based on the promised money, hiring a bigger staff, booking more trips, and expanding its outreach. It seemed like a sure-fire bet. Sheldon was the third richest man in America, with more than $30 billion, just behind Bill Gates and Warren Buffett.

But virtually all of his fortune was tied up in his company's stock. That stock, in turn, depended on highly fickle gambling revenues. In 2008, he lost 95 percent of his fortune. He canceled his yearly funding to Birthright. Since his money was critical, Birthright went into crisis, laying off staff and cutting back trips.

Today, Birthright is rebuilding its program, partly with help from the Israeli government. Mr. Adelson returned in 2011 with another big gift. But Birthright learned its lesson. It is now getting more of its donations in the form of small gifts from a large number of people, rather than in the form of giant gifts from a few of the ultra-rich.

"We learned that depending on one mega-donor isn't the best long-term strategy for a nonprofit," said Jacob Dallal, Birthright's communications chief. "We appreciate Mr. Adelson's generosity. But we also know we can't depend just on him."

Wealth Isn't All It's Cracked Up to Be

If there's one thing I've learned from my seven years of covering wealth, it's that being rich isn't all that great. Wealth doesn't solve our problems; it just creates different ones. While our culture celebrates the rich, we rarely see the personal sacrifices they made to get there: the broken marriages and alienated children, the health problems, the life devoted entirely to a business or idea.

Money is a great liberator. It can give us freedoms and choice. But the mountains of new research on wealth and happiness tells us that money only improves our lives to a point. After that, it's just numbers in a bank account. The lessons of high-beta wealth further support this research. If large wealth can't even give us stability and peace of mind, if there is no land of financial contentment but only a world of constant ups and downs and striving to preserve your fortune, then we might be able to put wealth in a more realistic perspective.

As Tim Blixseth once told me in 2006 (perhaps foretelling his own downfall), "No one really owns wealth. It doesn't mean anything by itself. It's just a tool, something we use for a while, and then it's someone else's."

A recent study funded by the Gates Foundation, called "The Joys and Dilemmas of Wealth," polled people worth $25 million or more and found that many had deep anxieties about money and their lives. Said one respondent:

> If we can get people just a little bit more informed, so they know that getting the $20 million or $200 million won't necessarily bring them all that they'd hoped for, then maybe they'd concentrate instead on things that would make the world a better place and could help to make them truly happy.

Again, these tips won't rid us of high-beta wealth or its contagion. But they might allow us to build better financial and psychological levees to protect us against the coming storms and floods.

In addition to the survival tips, however, there is also a lesson from high-beta wealth that might give us cause for hope for the future—and perhaps even partial redemption for the reputations of today's rich.

LIKE BUBBLES IN A VAT

In 2008, I stood on the front lawn of a bright orange mansion in Florida as the owners watched almost all of their possessions go up for auction. Their names were Richard and Amanda Peacock, and they had made millions in commercial real estate. But after getting buried with mortgage debt and medical bills, they were selling off more than a decade's worth of toys and status symbols.

"Four million, do I hear four and a half?" shouted the auctioneer, as he took bids for the 10,000-square-foot oceanside mansion. "Come on, people—the good Lord stopped making oceanfront property a long time ago."

The Peacocks were selling their 2004 Ferrari and five other cars, a motorcycle, an RV, two Jet Skis, and a room full of hunting trophies, including a stuffed wildebeast and an elephant head. They were even selling off their eight rare parrots. It was like a yard sale of the super-rich, where everything was up for sale.

Although the wildebeest sold ($250), most of the rest failed to meet the asking price. The top bid on the house, whose interior was heavy on gold and zebra skin, was $5.5 million, so the couple decided to try to hang on a few more months to see if the market improved.

Standing in the back of the auction tent was an older man and his son, both wearing white polo shirts and khakis. They were low bidders on almost everything. They were both jovial, tanned, and fit. And while they wouldn't reveal their names, they said they had been in the real estate business and got out in 2006 "when things felt overcooked." Now they were buying up distressed assets—whether it was mortgages, land, orange mansions, or rare parrots.

Pointing to a shiny yellow Lamborghini parked nearby, the son said: "I just bought that the other day from a dealer for 60 percent less than the sticker price," the son said. "It's brand-new."

While the Peacocks had clearly fallen off the wealth ladder, the father-son bargain hunters seemed to be on their way up. Economists and academics often write about the rich as a fixed group.

The chances of moving into the ranks of the rich, or falling out, seem increasingly remote.

"Wealth begets power, which begets more wealth," wrote economist Joseph Stiglitz in 2011, adding that America is comparable to Egypt, Yemen, and other oligarchies where wealth and power are controlled by a few families.

"The top one percent may complain about the kind of government we have in America, but in truth they like it just fine: too gridlocked to re-distribute, too divided to do anything but lower taxes," Stiglitz wrote.

Kevin Phillips wrote in *Wealth and Democracy* that the wealthiest families in America keep getting richer, with their wealth and power snowballing through the market's ups and downs and squashing opportunity for the rest of the country. "The early-twenty-first-century United States was not just the world's richest nation but had also become the West's citadel of inherited wealth. Aristocracy was a cultural and economic fact, if not a statutory one."

This is the dismal view, effectively stating that unless you're already rich, you have little chance of ever getting there. Despite our national dream of becoming a classless society, we have become a nation of enduring privilege.

Yet the Peacocks and the rise of high-beta wealth offer a more fluid version of wealth. The Peacocks of yesterday are being replaced by the bargain hunters and entrepreneurs of tomorrow. One millionaire is sliding down the wealth ladder while another is climbing up. We are not a hardened plutocracy but a nation of one-hit wonders and financial lottery winners who form an ever-changing group.

According to the IRS, America's top four hundred taxpayers in 2008 made an average of $271 million each in 2008. Yet nearly three-quarters of that group have appeared on the list only *once* since the IRS began tracking them in 1994. Only 12 percent of the four hundred appeared on the list twice, and only 1 percent appeared every year since 1994. The peak of the American income pyramid, in other words, is more like Mt. Everest—a height reached only briefly, and rarely more than once, by most people in their lifetimes.

The rich don't always fall far. And many of the rich just keep getting richer. Yet even the top 1 percent of American earners—or those with incomes of $380,000 or more in 2008—represent an ever-shifting group. One study showed that only half of the top 1 percenters made the cut more than once over a ten-year period.

We have become a nation of more disposable elites who live or die on the stock-market tickers that scroll across our TV screens and computer terminals every day. This moment in history is more like the industrial revolution of the 1800s, when fast-changing technologies created a roiling upper class that was in stark contrast to the more rigid class system of Europe.

"With no chartered aristocracy, and no law of entail, how can any family in America imposingly perpetuate itself?" wrote Herman Melville in his 1852 novel *Pierre, or The Ambiguities*. "In our cities families rise and burst like bubbles in a vat. For indeed, the democratic element operates as a subtle acid among us; forever producing new things by corroding the old."

Alexis de Tocqueville made a similar observation about the America of the 1800s, noting in his *Democracy in America* that "there is still a class of menials and a class of masters, but these classes are not always comprised of the same individuals, still less of the same families. And those who command are not more secure of perpetuity than those who obey."

Of course, the revolving-door elite of the industrial revolution and the Gilded Age gave way to the hyper-concentration of wealth and power in the 1920s. Whether our age of high-beta wealth ends the same way remains to be seen.

Yet, for now, the wealthy in America will rise and fall like the bubbles in Melville's vat. In their rising and popping lies opportunity—at least for those who understand the fleeting nature of today's wealth.

ACKNOWLEDGMENTS

I am indebted to the *Wall Street Journal* for giving me the tools and time to write this book. Ever since I started the wealth beat in 2004, my editors have shown extraordinary support in my efforts to chronicle the lives and culture of the new rich. They have been especially tolerant of my book writing and blogging habits. In particular, I am grateful to Robert Thomson, Mike Miller, Rebecca Blumenstein, Alan Murray, and Ken Brown, as well as my former *Journal* editors Nik Deogun and Jared Sandberg, for their help in securing a book leave and allowing me to return to my beat—arguably the best in all of journalism. Ken was especially kind in allowing me to extend my leave.

Thanks to my editor Francesco Guerrera and all my hardworking colleagues in Blogger's Cove for making the *Journal* a genuinely fun place to be.

John Mahaney and Tina Constable have made Crown a nurturing home for my books and ideas. A special thanks to John for his fast and insightful edits and for his gentle persistence in keeping me on deadline. Richard Pine is that rarest of agents, a dedicated advocate who also takes the long view.

Annik La Farge, one of the wisest and most generous souls in publishing, has repeatedly led me out of the woods while writing this book. On days when I felt stuck, Annik would cheer me up over croissants and tea at Bergamote and show me the way forward. Her comments and edits have vastly improved this book. Let's keep saving for that boat!

Eric Anderson is one of the best journalists I know, even if he's not officially in journalism. His story ideas, commitment to facts, and meticulous edits have proved invaluable to me. I am lucky to count him as a friend.

The wealthy subjects of this book have given me the one thing that their money can never buy: time. A special thanks to Jack Warner, Tim and Edra Blixseth, Jackie and David Siegel, Frank and Susan Kavanaugh, Mary Patrick, John McAfee, Leonard Stern, Brian and Basil Maher, and Donald Rubin for spending hours and hours answering my questions. Thanks to Ken Cage for letting me tag along for two days of repossessing planes and boats. Anthony Harris and Lloyd White have been gracious and generous in the way that only a butler can be. I admire your service hearts.

For their insights into wealth, I am continually indebted to Stephen Martiros, Peter Scaturro, Frances Aldrich Sevilla-Secasa, Keith Whitaker, George Walper, Russ Prince, and Maria Elena-Lagomasino.

Researchers Esme Deprez and Erin Geiger Smith unearthed articles, references, and data that I never could have found on my own.

To all my friends, I apologize for my long absences and unanswered e-mails over the past year. To Adam and Jen, Larry and Vicki, Jesse and Sarah, Dave Rothman, Chris, and Brad, thanks for sticking with me. David Gilmour has taught me what it means to be a true entrepreneur, and his energy, elegance, and ideas remain—for me—a model of enlightened wealth.

Perk Hixon and Marguerite Lee have been gracious guides and mentors since the day I started the wealth beat. We look forward to that rarest of Manhattan bonds: friends who are also building neighbors.

Betty and her fellow Sundowners remain among my most loyal supporters.

To Dad and Kathi, who raised me to care more about ideas than money, I am forever grateful. Most of all, I am indebted to my wife, Rebecca, without whom I could never have done this book. She gave up her weekends and vacations for a year and a half so I could write—all while juggling her own sixty-hour-a-week job, two kids, and multiple side duties. Through it all she remains the picture of beauty, grace, and intelligence.

My daughters, Amelia and Elana, have encouraged me every day by asking, "Is the book done yet?" Yes, girls, the book is done.

NOTES

INTRODUCTION: GIVING UP THE GULFSTREAM

P. 9: BY 2007, THERE WERE MORE THAN TEN MILLION MILLIONAIRE HOUSEHOLDS Federal Reserve Surveys of Consumer Finance.

P. 9: THE COMBINED ANNUAL INCOMES OF THE TOP 1 PERCENT Facundo Alvaredo, Tony Atkinson, Thomas Piketty, and Emmanuel Saez, Top Incomes Database.

P. 10: IN THE EIGHTEEN-MONTH PERIOD BETWEEN THE END OF 2007 Specterem Group.

P. 10: INCOMES FOR THE TOP 1 PERCENT OF EARNERS Jonathan A. Parker and Annette Vissing-Jorgensen, "The Increase in Income Cyclicality of High-Income Households and Its Relation to the Rise in Top Income Shares," Northwestern University, September 7, 2010.

CHAPTER 1: WHO REPO'D MY YACHT?

P. 26: HE TRAVELS AT A MOMENT'S NOTICE Marc Weingarten, "The Learjet Repo Man," Salon.com, June 6, 2009; Sean Silcoff, "Foreclosing on a Plane, Then Flying It Away," New York Times, March 13, 2009.

P. 26: BETWEEN 1995 AND 2010, THE NUMBER OF PRIVATE JETS *JPMorgan Business Jet Monthly*, June 3, 2010.

P. 26: JEFF HENDERSON, A MICHIGAN-BASED "Economic Tide Is Rising for Repo Man," *New York Times*, May 20, 2008.

P. 27: MINNESOTA AUTO DEALER DENNY HECKER Dee Depass, "Hecker Lists $767 Million in Debt; Bankruptcy Filing Tells Tale of Spending and Debt," *Star Tribune* (Minneapolis, MN), July 3, 2009.

P. 27: "THERE IS A CERTAIN TYPE OF AFFLUENT CUSTOMER" Joel Schechtman, "A Pawnshop for the Affluent," *Newsweek*, October 28, 2010.

CHAPTER 2: 1982: THE MAGIC YEAR FOR WEALTH

P. 40: IT WAS MORE LIKE THE DARKNESS BEFORE THE DAWN "1982 Year in Review," UPI.com.

P. 40: AS KEVIN PHILLIPS, THE POLITICAL COMMENTATOR Kevin Phillips, *Wealth and Democracy* (New York: Random House, 2002), 132.

P. 42: DURING THE CONSUMER-LED EXPANSION OF THE 1950S Facundo Alvaredo, Tony Atkinson, Thomas Piketty, and Emmanuel Saez, Top Incomes Database.

P. 42: THE ELITE WERE EQUALLY RESTRAINED Edward N. Wolff, *Top Heavy: The Increasing Inequality of Wealth in America and What Can Be Done About It* (New York: New Press, 2002), 9.

P. 42: IN 1955, ONLY 276 PEOPLE Larry Samuel, *Rich: The Rise and Fall of American Wealth Culture* (New York: AMACOM, 2009), 121.

P. 42: IN 1982, HALF OF THE MEMBERS OF THE *FORBES* 400 Phillips, *Wealth and Democracy*.

P. 42: IN THAT SAME YEAR, THERE WERE ONLY THIRTEEN BILLIONAIRES Peter W. Bernstein and Annalyn Swan, eds., *All the Money in the World: How the Forbes 400 Make—and Spend—Their Fortunes* (New York: Knopf, 2007), 65.

P. 43: *SCIENCE DIGEST* OBSERVED Samuel, *Rich*.

P. 43: AN ARTICLE IN THE *NEW YORK TIMES* "Palm Beach Calm Oasis of Wealthy," *New York Times*, March 21, 1982.

P. 43: *TIME* MAGAZINE IN 1982 NAMED THE COMPUTER Otto Friedrich, "The Computer," *Time*, January 4, 1983.

P. 44: "THE SERVICES OF THE BEST PERFORMERS" Robert H. Frank and Philip J. Cook, *The Winner-Take-All-Society* (New York: Penguin, 1996).

P. 44: IN 1981, RONALD REAGAN PERSUADED CONGRESS Congressional Budget Office.

P. 45: IN *THE SNOWBALL* Alice Schroeder, *The Snowball: Warren Buffett and the Business of Life* (New York: Bantam, 2008), 436.

P. 45: BY 1986, MANY OF THE COUNTRY'S TOP ONE HUNDRED EARNERS Phillips, *Wealth and Democracy*, 140.

P. 47: THE TOP NETWORK TV SHOW Top TV shows, 1982, The '80s Server.

P. 48: THE LIST RECALLED THE FABLED "FOUR HUNDRED" Bernstein and Swan, eds., *All the Money in the World*, 238.

P. 48: TEXAS HAD SIXTY-FIVE RESIDENTS ON THE 1982 LIST Ibid., 65.

P. 49: IN 1981, THE TOP 1 PERCENT HAD 8 PERCENT OF THE NATION'S INCOME Facundo Alvaredo, Tony Atkinson, Thomas Piketty, and Emmanuel Saez, Top Incomes Database.

P. 49: IN 1981, THERE WERE ABOUT 638,000 MILLIONAIRES Internal Revenue Service, "Trends in Personal Wealth 1976–1981."

P. 52: IN TWO YEARS, HE HAD $400 MILLION UNDER MANAGEMENT Robert Frank, "Now, Mutual Funds Under Fire—Charges Against Canary Capital Cast a Spotlight on the Sterns; A Journey from Hartz to Hedge," *Wall Street Journal*, September 4, 2003.

P. 52: IN 2000, WHEN THE S&P 500 FELL 9 PERCENT Peter Elkind, Christopher Tkaczyk, and Doris Burke, "The Secrets of Eddie Stern," *Fortune*, April 19, 2004.

P. 54: THE STERNS ARE PART OF WHAT John Bellamy Foster, "The Financialization of Accumulation," *The Monthly Review*, October 1, 2010.

P. 56: AS WE NOTED EARLIER, THE TOP 1 PERCENT OF EARNERS Parker and Vissing-Jorgensen, "Increase in Income Cyclicality."

P. 56: A STUDY OF PAY FOR ALL CEOS Steven N. Kaplan, "Some Facts About CEO Pay and Corporate Governance," 2011.

P. 57: BETWEEN 2008 AND 2010 Spectrem Group.

P. 58: AT THE VERY TOP, THE LOSSES DURING DOWNTURNS Duncan Greenberg, "America's Biggest Billionaire Losers of 2008," *Forbes*, December 6, 2008.

NOTES

P. 60: HIS EFFORTS TO EXPAND WERE SOON BLOCKED "History," Waterfront Commission of New York Harbor, WCNYH.org.

P. 61: IN THE MID-1950S, PORT NEWARK SERVED "The Container Industry: The World in a Box," *Economist*, March 16, 2006.

CHAPTER 3: HOMES LIKE WHITE ELEPHANTS

P. 73: IN LAS VEGAS, MORE THAN A QUARTER OF THE MANSIONS John Gittelsohn, "Wealthy Leaving Las Vegas Mansions as Foreclosures Spreading," Bloomberg.com, April 26, 2011.

P. 73: THE SHARE OF THEIR FORTUNES DEVOTED TO REAL ESTATE Arthur B. Kennickell, "Ponds and Streams: Wealth and Income in the U.S., 1989 to 2007," Finance and Discussion Series, Division of Research and Statistics and Monetary Affairs, Federal Reserve Board, Washington, D.C., January 7, 2009.

P. 73: A RUSSIAN BILLIONAIRE IN GREENWICH Robert Frank, "Greenwich Mansion Planned with 26 Toilets," *The Wealth Report* (Blog), April 22, 2008.

CHAPTER 4: LUCKY'S LANDING

P. 93: JACK WARNER WAS A "MIDDLE-CLASS MILLIONAIRE" Russ Alan Prince and Lewis Schiff, *The Middle-Class Millionaire: The Rise of the New Rich and How They Are Changing America* (New York: Currency/Doubleday, 2008).

P. 94: A STUDY OF AMERICANS WITH $1.5 MILLION OR MORE *Barclays Wealth*, "The Age Illusion: How the Wealthy Are Redefining Retirement." *Barclay's Wealth*, September 2010.

CHAPTER 5: THE MAKE-BELIEVE BILLIONAIRE

P. 109: IN THE 1980S, TIM'S BUSINESS CRASHED Scott McMillion, "Past Plagues Taylor Ranch Bidder," *Denver Post*, January 8, 1994.

P. 116: "SHE HAS BEEN RECKLESSLY SPENDING MONEY AS IF IT GROWS ON TREES" "Yellowstone Club Founder Speaks Out," PR Newswire, June 15, 2009.

NOTES

P. 120: HE TOLD *FAST COMPANY* "Plagued by lawsuits, McAfee Founder Hunts for Cures in Belize," Jeff Wise, *Fast Company*, May 1, 2010.

P. 120: IN 2008, THE *NEW YORK TIMES* RAN AN ARTICLE David Leonhardt and Geraldine Fabrikant, "Rise of the Super-Rich Hits a Sobering Wall," *New York Times*, August 20, 2009.

CHAPTER 6: BIG MONEY RUINS EVERYTHING

P. 130: THE PAEPCKES VACATIONED ON A LARGE RANCH Ted Conover, "Lives Well Lived: Elizabeth Paepcke; Eve in the Garden of Aspen," *New York Times*, January 1, 1995.

P. 133: THERE WAS ALSO, OF COURSE, THE APPEAL F. Scott Fitzgerald, *The Great Gatsby* (New York: Scribner, 2004 [1925]), 5.

P. 134: THE *ASPEN DAILY NEWS*, IN ITS APRIL FOOL'S ISSUE Robert Frank, "The Billionaire and the Bookstore: Sam Wyly Buys Left-Leaning Aspen Landmark," *Wall Street Journal*, October 5, 2007.

P. 139: "OUR JOB IS TO WELCOME THESE VISITORS TO TOWN" Susan Greene, "'Big Money' Song Draws Aspen Skiing Co.'s Ill Will," *Denver Post*, January 12, 2010.

P. 140: THE ASPEN SKI CO. TOLD DAN Scott Condon, "Aspen Skico: Mistake Made in Firing of Musician," *Aspen Times* (Aspen, Colorado), January 8, 2010.

CHAPTER 7: GIVING JEEVES THE PINK SLIP

P. 153: "THE CONSUMPTION OF HIGH-CONSUMPTION HOUSEHOLDS" Jonathan A. Parker and Annette Vissing-Jorgensen, "Who Bears Aggregate Fluctuations and How?" January 2009.

P. 153: "THEIR SPENDING BEHAVIOR IS A LOT MORE VOLATILE" Ajay Kapur, Mirae Asset Management, "The Global Investigator; Michael Moore, Misrepresentation and Migrating Plutonomies," October 7, 2009.

P. 157: IN OTHER WORDS, THE FEW MILLION AMERICANS AT THE TOP Robert Frank, "U.S. Economy Is Increasingly Tied to the Rich," *Wall Street Journal*, August 5, 2010.

CHAPTER 8: WHAT'S WRONG WITH CALIFORNIA?

P. 174: CAPITAL GAINS REALIZATIONS TRIPLED Elizabeth Hill and Bradley Williams, "California's Changing Income Distribution," Legislative Analyst's Office, State of California, August 2000.

P. 175: BY 1998, THE TOP 1 PERCENT OF EARNERS IN CALIFORNIA Ibid.

P. 177: WHEN THE DOT-COM BUBBLE BURST Jacob M. Schlesinger and Bryan Gruley, "Main Street: A Tale of a Broker and His Clients and an Era's End," *Wall Street Journal*, December 27, 2002.

P. 181: IN NEW YORK, THE TOP 1 PERCENT PAY Interview with Donald J. Boyd, senior fellow at the Nelson A. Rockefeller Institute of Government, February 2011.

P. 182: IN A REPORT DOWNGRADING NEW JERSEY'S CREDIT RATING S&P, Global Credit Portal, Ratings Direct, New Jersey General Obligation, February 9, 2011.

P. 185: THE COMMISSION RECOMMENDED LOWERING TAX RATES Commission on the 21st Century Economy, press release, September 29, 2009.

EPILOGUE

P. 205: LINKEDIN'S FOUNDER—Robert Frank, "Reid Hoffman Is Silicon Valley's Newest Billionaire," *The Wealth Report* (blog), May 19, 2011, http://blogs.wsj.com.

P. 206: BY THE END OF 2010—Mark Zandi, Moody's Analytics, Personal Outlays by Income 2010, q3.

P. 207: AS THE GLOBAL INVESTOR—Lauren Rublin, "Buy Low, Stay Nimble," *Barron's*, June 11, 2011.

P. 209: ALAN GREENSPAN—CNBC Transcript, Alan Greenspan on CNBC's *Squawk Box*, July 1, 2010.

P. 210: ERIC LEFTKOFSKY—Robert Frank, "How to Earn $4 Billion on Coupons," *Wall Street Journal*, June 4, 2011.

P. 211: IN HIS 2009 BOOK—Thomas J. Stanley, *Stop Acting Rich . . . and Start Acting Like a Real Millionaire* (John Wiley & Sons, 2009), 11.

P. 214: A RECENT STUDY—Graeme Wood, "Secret Fears of the Super Rich," *Atlantic*, April 2011.

P. 216: KEVIN PHILLIPS WROTE IN—*Wealth and Democracy,* 110.

P. 217: "THE TOP 1 PERCENT"—Joseph Stiglitz, "Of the 1 Percent, by the 1 Percent, for the 1 Percent," *Vanity Fair,* May 2011.

P. 217: "WITH NO CHARTERED"—Herman Meville, *Pierre: or the Ambiguities* (New York: Harper & Brothers, 1852), 9.

P. 217: "ALEXIS DE TOCQUEVILLE"—Alexis de Tocqueville, *Democracy in America* (D. Appleton & Co.), 668, 1092, 1835.

INDEX

Biltmore House, Asheville,
North Carolina, 81
Birthright, 212–213
Blixseth, Edra, 3–8, 10, 11, 17,
101–119, 121, 191
Blixseth, Tim, 1–5, 7, 8, 11,
105–118, 191, 214
Boats and yachts, 25–27, 31–39,
109
Boca Raton, Florida, 73
Boomerang Lending, 27
Boston Scientific Corporation, 59
Brady Bunch, The (television
show), 166
Branson, Richard, 119
Breckenridge, Colorado, 131
Bucksbaum family, 12, 146–147
Buffett, Warren, 45, 212
Burry, Michael, 195
Bush, George, 4
Bush, Jeb, 75
Butlers, 158–171, 207

Cage, Ken, 23–26, 28–39, 85, 207
Calendar Group, 166
California, economy in, 18,
172–186, 207, 210
"California's Changing Income
Distribution" (Williams),
176–177
Canary Capital Partners, 52, 53
Canary Investment
Management, 52
Capital gains, 174, 177–179, 209,
210
Caribou Club, Aspen, Colorado,
134
Cars, 4, 7, 8, 26, 80, 184, 193,
202, 215

CDOs, 195
Census Bureau, 58, 183
Cheslock, Dorothea, 74
Cheslock, Stanley, 74
Chrysler Financial, 27, 29
Cleverly, Michael, 132, 133, 144
Cole, Adam, 56
Computers, 43, 61
Connecticut, tax rates in,
181–182
Consumer Expenditure Survey,
152
Consumer spending habits, 19,
152–157, 170, 171
Cook, Philip J., 44
Coulter, Ann, 134
Craft, Randy, 23–26, 31–34,
37–39
Crawford, Jack, 126, 132–133
Credit Suisse, 112, 113, 115, 116,
195, 196
Crystal Island Ranch, Aspen,
Colorado, 135
Culture wars of 1960s, 43
Curiel, Dessire, 126
Curto, Joe, 61

Dallal, Jacob, 213
Dallas (television show), 47
Dana Point, California, 202
David-Weill, Michel, 45
Democracy in America
(Tocqueville), 217
Dent, Harry, 194
Denver, John, 141
Denver Post, 139
Deregulation, 43, 44
Deutsch Bank, 62
Disney World, 78

ABOUT THE AUTHOR

ROBERT FRANK is the author of the *New York Times* bestseller *Richistan: A Journey Through the American Wealth Boom and the Lives of the New Rich*. He covers wealth for the *Wall Street Journal* and writes *The Wealth Report*, a daily blog named one of the most influential financial blogs by *Time* magazine. Robert has been with the *Wall Street Journal* for eighteen years, covering Wall Street and serving as a foreign correspondent in London and Singapore. He lives in New York City with his wife and two daughters.